NO GAY OUT

AMERICAN ZEALOT

Book II

NO GAY OUT

AMERICAN ZEALOT

Book II

Don Drake

Planet Buddha Media
PO Box 23921
Eugene, Oregon 97402

Published in the U.S.A.

Library of Congress Cataloging-in Publication Data
Drake, Don
No Gay Out / American Zealot Book II / Don Drake
230 pages 12.7 x 20.32 cm
ISBN-13: 978-0692518182
ISBN-10: 0692518185

Book Design by D. Crow & S. Rowe

"It is no measure of health to be well adjusted to a profoundly sick society" — J. Krishnamurti

For

Jean-Paul

Table
of Contents

1 Metropolis   1

2 Inferno   21

3 Culture Shock   32

4 Vision Quest   64

5 Angry Gods   87

6 Jacob and Janet 106

7 Jacob's Wrestling Match   125

8 Preacher Boy   138

9 Lone Star   147

10 The End   157

11 Apocalypse   163

12 The Gay Science   194

13 Ecce Homo   220

1
Metropolis

Jacob's dad was well to do. Retired though he'd been forced to become, he'd still stroll daily to the local brokerage firm, enjoying the non-stop motion of the ticker and the talking heads on the large screens. He'd gab with brokers and move his tens and hundreds of thousands around in a perpetual game of day trading. That was his idea of fun. Other than those routine jaunts, Jacob's dad'd be home swigging martinis or scotch on the rocks. He'd be shit faced by evening, and mean.

Then he'd start waxing nostalgic in soliloquies about his glory days. Days when he'd closed this deal for the company, or when that deal went through grinding all competitors to dust. Just replays, rewinds, and rehashes of events so far gone that they were nothing more than recollections of fragments of fragmentary dreams, mental will o' the wisps, thought-garbage fit for oblivion and in need of serious expunging. But he was hanging on to them, dramatizing the events, recounting them as if they were conquests of a world class history maker. Death being the great equalizer, when all's said and done, even the biggest movers and shakers of human history go back to the same ol' dust. In the meantime though, Jacob couldn't take much more of his dad's fucked up bullshit.

He'd had about enough of his incessant palaver night after fucking night. The drunken monologues eventually turned belligerent and downright nasty; 'abusive' being the technical term. Jacob finally started dropping the F-bomb during his dad's yelling and blustering. One evening, he just couldn't take it anymore and he just exploded at his dad. His father seemed astonished at first but settled into it rather quickly, as if he'd been expecting the outburst for some time. At first, Jacob felt pretty bad about it so he later apologized. Even though he loathed him, he couldn't stand the thought of hurting his father's feelings by showing such terrible disrespect. However, any reconciliation or forgiveness was momentary. Pejoratives and expletives had officially become a part of their mutual vocabulary. The father pretty much hated his bohemian son, and the angry teenage son pretty much hated his fucked up father. A man who didn't even have the core decency to pretend to be a real father. The guy was simply incapable. He was just an overgrown ten-year old boy in the body of a sixty-five year old retired ex-company-man geezer, and that, as far as Jacob was concerned, was about the size of it.

His brother Mitch on the other hand, was the golden child. He was younger than Jacob by almost six years. There was a definite generation gap there already, and not much of a bridge to cross it because while Jacob was an avid reader and voracious self-learner, his little brother Mitch liked the more common, banal things like sports and heavy metal. They were worlds apart with respect to time and personality.

His father had always been disdainful of him, even when he was just a baby. Maybe there was too much facial resemblance; something about Jacob reminded his dad too much of himself. He was a self-hater. But Mitch, that glorious handsome kid, that boy, why, "he's a beaut like his mother. Yessiree, he's a decent, normal kid. Not like that nervous nelly, his older brother, the bookworm neurotic. The dreamer. The shit's head is up in the clouds when it's not up his own ass. He's no good."

Their mom was a passive woman. She took her husband's guff like the good old fashioned wife that she was, a trophy wife — she'd won the Miss Seattle beauty pageant back in the day — yes, a silent wallflower, behaved as wives should, as they're expected to. That's how she'd been brought up by her old fashioned parents in an old fashioned home with good old fashioned values.

And speaking of values, Jacob — and hence his brother Mitch — were brought up with somewhat conflicting ones. Although they went to a private Christian school, were taught about the bible and Jesus and all that stuff that everybody is supposed to know, that everybody believes, the family wasn't all too religious except in superficial ways. Merely paying lip service to the lord god almighty thou who art in heaven. Jacob's hotshot dad's devotion to god was unctuous at best; he never went to church like everybody was supposed to, though he talked about it a lot, about how great god was and all that. That's because his dad's true loyalty was to his company. He was a bona fide, dyed in the wool company man first, an investor second, a man of charismatic charm third, and family-man dash religious-man somewhere nebulously in last place, if at all. Wife and family were his professional props; family men with children were stable, god fearing decent folk, the backbone of the nation. Mitch just happened to be a perk that came out of the otherwise pesky prop, for the younger boy was the apple, as they say, of his father's eye.

Summer vacation. Tenth grade, high school. Fuck school.

Jacob hated it. He loathed the private Christian school in Seattle he'd attended from first through 8th grade, as well as its annexed high school. It was located somewhat on the outskirts of the sprawling city. He'd been chauffeured to and from it in the family limo five days a week for years. The high school routine wasn't much different: daily prayers before classes, bible study, the occasional church services, and pious convocations. Being a pretty sharp kid, Jacob had gotten the gist of the whole religion thing. He believed in god. He thought Jesus was just alright like his dad did. But much more deeply than his dad — believed that god's hand was in everything. He was a peculiar kid.

He'd been taking solace in his personal conversations with god ever since he was little. His god would talk back to him, with the voice of a much older man that he'd hear in his head. He imagined it, knew he did, and yet a part of him believed that it was the authentic voice of god, that somehow there was no difference. It didn't matter to him either way. He lived in a private world, his own *sanctum sanctorum*, meeting with his father's disapproval from early on. His father was a practical man, a businessman, but his son Jacob, why, he was "a rebellious gypsy, a dreamer. Thinks money grows on trees like bananas on a tropical island."

He didn't have a whole lotta friends, had a select few very close friends — boys and girls — but he wasn't at the bottom of the social barrel either. He sorta flew under the radar overall, didn't get too involved. Conventional teachers paid no attention to him, he didn't go the extra mile to impress them or try to get their approval. He didn't want to be noticed. He liked to read, study, draw comics, learn stuff; he liked books a lot. But he wasn't a nerd type either. He wasn't athletic, but was no waif; he wasn't the target of bullies, even though one could find quite a few of those types lumbering everywhere.

Though he talked to god and prayed in his own way, he wasn't religious. He hated the whole damn thing pretty much, especially the petty moralities and dreadful stories. Just couldn't wrap his head around stuff like "Happy shall he be, that taketh and dasheth thy little ones against the stones," and a whole lotta other batshit crazy stuff people took to be gospel, so to speak. He mocked religious holidays and church on Sundays; even told a religious friend of his that it was all bullshit, to his buddy's swooning dismay. He was a bit of a provocateur, even in middle school. Peers thought, whenever they did take notice of him, that he was kinda interesting.

But as middle school was coming to a close, hormonal surges started intensifying. Jacob'd been playing with his pee-nis ever since he was around four or five years of age. He pictured naked boys in his mind, and that excited him. The thrill of thinking of them persisted through the end of middle school, but not for a second did it occur to him to act on it. Just fantasy was all. His buddies at school wouldn't have approved, because all they talked about was which girls were hot and which were not. Just to fit in, of course, Jacob pretended and said oh yeah, she's hot and all that kind of macho stuff. He was capable of enough objectivity to empathize, as much as he possibly could, with their perspectives and aesthetics.

Still, there was a subtle barrier. He was unaware of it at first, but it only got fortified, reinforced and more cumbersome the older he got. Nearing the end of his Freshman year, in preparation for the remaining years of high school and all its hormonal pitfalls, a special three-hour seminar was held about the perils of homosexuality. The seminar was being sponsored by a local "secular" — as they designated themselves — conversion-therapy organization. A PG-rated affair, strictly voluntary, for parents and their children.

Jacob's dad read the flier that had come in the mail, and was all for it. Of course, he himself couldn't attend due to business meetings, but Jacob would go with his mom. His mom agreed but Jacob wasn't keen on the idea. Something about it made him feel queasy, uneasy. Because the seminar was about those people — and it seemed to focus more on males — who thought people of the same sex were hot, and how unnatural that was.

As far as Jacob was concerned, it was as natural as breathing oxygen. There was no effort involved. He'd think of some girls. Not hot. He'd think of some boys. Hot. And that was pretty much all there was to it. But he'd learned early on directly or by osmosis from his peers, and even from his teachers at school, that it was unnatural for him to feel excited about boys. Boys frequently used the words fag, queer, and gay as simple put downs. Jacob himself had used those words thinking nothing of it at the time. He simply hadn't connected the dots.

But a picture was beginning to emerge, and it seemed to be a rather looming, big picture, bigger than the circle of his peers, bigger than the faculty of his school, bigger than the educational system itself. It was a societal picture. And with respect to society, it entailed culture, history, and traditions. And of course, religion. That religion, of course, was Judeo-christian based. Which meant that god was involved in it.

Although this big picture had started concretizing slowly over the years, it had remained somewhat ambiguous. Until the seminar.

The presentation was conducted by three men. There was a main speaker and two "witnesses" who attested to the fact that they had once been homosexual but had victoriously reclaimed their heterosexuality through various scientific methods. Although he'd had his reservations, Jacob was indeed curious about what the three men had to say. He wanted to know why being attracted to people of the same sex was worthy of all the bluster and time it took to create a symposium about it.

The main dude got up to welcome the parents and students. Surprisingly the turn out at the gym was huge, as if every single ninth grade *boy* and his parents had showed up. There was only a smattering of girls. Okay so, the seminar was — quite obviously, — geared to males. Which made Jacob wonder if homosexuality was mostly a male issue; indeed, he also wondered: *is* there such a thing as a homosexual? If such people did in fact exist, something would have to be seriously wrong with them. Could *he* be one of them?

He fantasized about nude boys. About two or three of them in his class. When he masturbated, he would climax to the thought of Wade smiling, Wade joking, Wade talking to his classmates. Wade was on his mind quite often, but he'd thought nothing of it. Wade would simply enter his thoughts during blissful orgasmic absorption, but other than that, Wade was just Wade. Another boy. Another beautiful, shining boy.

But, Jacob thought, that didn't necessarily mean that he was attracted to Wade. After all, he was not a homosexual. Homosexuals suffer because of their abnormality, at least that was the impression he got from everything and everyone hitherto. That was apparently the perspective of the men holding the seminar as well. But Jacob wasn't suffering. He didn't feel abnormal. Therefore, he wasn't homosexual.

Couldn't be.

The main guy introduced the two "witnesses" by name. All three waved at the crowd with a smile; referring to themselves as success stories. They put the parents' minds at ease, reiterated that the short conference was "rated PG," allaying any worries with a disclaimer that what they were about to speak of or share would in no way be explicit or provocative.

The first order of business was to explain that they were not a religious organization, although many on the staff were Christian. The leader related his personal story for the sake of the high school Freshmen.

"At the end of middle school, yes, I was your age once, I find it hard to believe it myself —" a few guffaws — "I had no idea what high school had in store for me. You could say I was thrown into the jungle to fend for myself. The world seemed like such a crazy place. I went through a very tough time, especially after I hit puberty." More snickering.

Jacob listened carefully, not quite knowing what to expect.

"Hindsight is 20/20 as they say. That's very true. Now that I think about it, if I'd had the opportunity to attend a seminar like this one and had been informed like you will be today, my life could've gone much more smoothly. I might not have had to deal with anger and depression. I might not have attempted suicide."

He lifted his wrists up over his head for the audience to see. A silent pause as he hung his head, chin to chest, arms raised high. The audience gasped. There were visibly large vertical gashes up both his wrists. The dramatic act had impact, it was a shocker. Might've ventured boldly right into PG-13 territory even.

He brought his wrists down and looked up again.

"All the bullying, abuse, name calling and beatings."

Jacob wondered why he hadn't just said 'fuck it' and dropped out.

"I attended the only public school in my neighborhood. No private school options like all you lucky kids have. I went to a very large public high school with hundreds of students. For me, it was a huge nightmare."

Jacob gulped. It was getting weird real fast.

"I was not particularly frail, or non-athletic. You could say I was quite an average kid all around, by the looks of me. There was nothing outstanding about the way I looked, and as you may already know, high school is all about appearances. There wasn't anything unusual enough about my appearance that would warrant the bullying I endured. Bullying to such an unbearable extent that I was driven to slashing my wrists one night in the bathtub. Please don't misunderstand me, I'm not saying that someone's appearance or anything at all for that matter, should ever, and I mean *ever*, warrant bullying in any shape or form. What I want you to think about however, is the sociological reality, or rather, the social situation that would bring such bullying upon me. Why? I was just a normal looking kid, so why did I get picked on more than anybody else?"

Everybody was very quiet. The parents of course knew this was just a rhetorical question.

"Unfortunately, I happened to tell my closest childhood friend — he was a boy —, that I'd had a crush on one of the most popular guys in the school. A star athlete — of course — who everybody admired, even the teachers. Obviously I wasn't the only person to have a crush on him, but I made the terrible mistake of confessing it to my so-called best friend.

"At first he thought I was joking around. When he realized I wasn't, it really freaked him out. He called me all kinds of names, said he didn't know I was a *fag*, and that as of that moment we weren't friends anymore. Well, it was my turn to think he was kidding around, but he wasn't. I was devastated. I'm sure you can guess what happened next. The very next day, he told our other friends, both boys and girls, about my confession. That I was attracted to a guy."

Parents sat looking dumbfounded, not knowing what to think. Jacob looked around him, checking the faces on his fellow students. Couldn't get a read on any of them, except one of the jock's had a smirk on his face.

"My parents didn't have a clue about my attraction to boys. My best friend hadn't known either. And to tell you the truth — and this happened when I was a Freshman, ninth grade — I don't think I even thought twice about my attraction to those of the same sex. I was unaware. I thought it was perfectly normal, I didn't think anything of it. I just didn't talk about crushes, in general because I felt embarrassed. You'd feel the same way if you had a crush on a member of the opposite sex too, wouldn't you?

"You could say I was 'hormonally challenged,' in more ways than one. But the reality of my situation really hit home when the best friend I'd grown up with called me a fag, ended our friendship, and spread the word at school that I was a *homo*. Obviously he was mitigating the possibility of being held guilty by association. His survival instincts kicked in. After all, we were best friends. He'd had enough sense to know that if anyone at school even *thought* you had feelings you shouldn't have for those of the same sex, you'd basically be signing your own death warrant.

"Now I'm not saying all high schools are like that, especially in this day and age. Students have become more educated about homosexuality, and have become more tolerant than back in my day.

"But —" he paused dramatically, looking down at the stage as if suddenly saddened "— is that a good thing? Of course it's good that there is less bullying today. However, too much tolerance leads to acceptance, acceptance to curiosity and before you know it, the promotion of homosexuality. Like a virus running rampant through an otherwise healthy society.

Parents nodded, as did some students.

That's why our organization is here. For young people who are confused. Our principles are based on sound scientific research. Homosexuality is learned or preferential behavior. For example, it can be activated at a very young and impressionable age by sexual abuse at the hands of a sibling, a relative, a family friend, or a complete stranger. Or it could be the result of some other kind of psychological trauma that occurred at a very early age. But we know one thing for sure. Homosexual behavior is a choice. That's why we're here, to steer confused young people, even confused older, middle aged, or even elderly people, in the right direction, so they can reclaim their masculinity if they are male, or femininity if they are female. We help people reclaim their manhood or womanhood, converting them back to their original, real biological sexual orientation."

Jacob's palms were sweating. He felt a knot in his stomach, felt nauseous. What kind of trauma had *he* suffered? Had he been sexually abused by somebody, and just blocked out the memory? As far as he knew, no such thing had ever happened. What horrible thing could possibly have happened to knock him off his *real* sexual orientation? Because one thing was crystal clear to Jacob. He realized he was exactly like the speaker. And he sure as shit didn't want to get bullied up one side and down the other like that guy had been. Thank god there were people like him in the world willing to tell their stories; trying to make a difference. At least now he knew that he must never, and that means *ever*, let on to anybody about his sexual thoughts about boys — and only boys. Thank you Mister Speaker for this invaluable, life saving piece of information.

There was a very slight, cool drizzle outside when the conference let out. The Pacific oceanic air was clean and refreshing. It was past twilight, downtown city lights were twinkling on the skyline. As they filed out of the gym, smirking jock — Jacob had never seen him before, must be a Freshman asshole from another school in the district — glanced at him with hostility. The boy, about twice Jacob's size, trounced past him as people were streaming out of the door; the boy's arm made contact with his. The jock's weight and momentum knocked Jacob into the doorjamb.

The big fella just kept lumbering forward, disappeared into the parking lot. Jacob looked at his mother, who didn't say a word about the incident. But that's how she was, extremely passive.

"Did you see what that asshole just did?" Jacob asked his mother.

"No," she said, though she did.

"I think he thinks I'm a fag," Jacob said.

His mom chuckled, but there was no further reaction or comment.

They drove into Seattle proper; decided on their usual family destination for dinner, a large refectory franchise, its bar and dining area always packed with urbanites. Jacob loved going there, ordered his usual club sandwich and a glass of iced tea. His mom ordered a Caesar salad. Jacob looked around while his mother grabbed her compact mirror to reapply her lipstick. A few booths over he saw one of his friends waving at him; she was there with her family. She hadn't been to the conversion therapy seminar. Jacob smiled and waved back.

Mother and son sat in silence, each immersed in their respective thoughts. They ate their food, again in silence, occasionally glancing about. His friend came to the table and asked if Jacob would like to join her and her family for a movie. Mother said of course.

Jacob loved Seattle in the morning, afternoon, and night. Its ambience, style, and culture. Its aesthetic sensibility and its liberal people. There was diversity. His school didn't reflect any of the city it inhabited, strangely enough, and maybe that's why he hated it so damn much — not to mention the religious thrust of it — even though he'd been used to it, having been there since before he could barely remember. He was all smiles with his friend and her family that misty, drizzly night. They were a pretty family, well groomed, well dressed, polite, funny, educated, intelligent, cultured. His friend was an aspiring ballerina, he'd gone to see her perform bit parts as a snowflake and so on in the Nutcracker every Christmas. Several families together enjoying food and conversation afterward, everybody dressed to the nines. There was warmth, laughter, sophistication. Even Jacob's dad seemed happy at those events, had the ability to make people laugh.

Yes, he loved his home city, his life there. The whole atmosphere, the mood, the feel of the place, the weather, the ocean breeze, all that it richly afforded the senses. Seattle made him feel vibrant and full of hope. There were also the occasional theophanies of beautiful young almost-men here and there, amidst the crowd, at the shopping center, the theaters, the stadium, restaurants, and hotel lounges. They were the icing on the cake that was Seattle, for it was their very presence that imbued it with reasons to live.

After he was dropped off at home, Jacob quickly went to his room to take a shower in his own private bathroom. It had been a long day. First school, then the strangeness of the after-school conversion-therapy seminar, then dinner, then the movies. But all in all it was a fine day, except for the jock fucker and the disturbing aftertaste of the I've-been-converted-and-so-can-you presentation. But Jacob wasn't too worried because, after all, he was still a virgin, and all he did was fantasize. About boys. So what. It'd probably pass, just a juvenile pubescent thing, a phase most likely. He was a normal kid, like any other kid. He was no "fag", no way.

What he got from the seminar was that something could trigger the homosexual urge in you instead of the so-called natural sexual urge, but that it was possible to course-correct it. And if you didn't, angry men would kick the living shit out of you. As far as he knew, he couldn't think of anything in particular that had set him on the abnormal — a term that one of the speakers had used — track, it felt perfectly natural to him, even though just a phase it was. Although he tried to visualize girls, they didn't do a thing for him, not at this stage in his life; so he couldn't conceive of how a course correction could take place. The most important thing he learned from the three converted, post-homosexual men: he didn't want to get beat up for this awkward phase he was going through. He appreciated the fact that none of them cited the biblical reasons why one shouldn't have homosexual urges, but at the same time, he wondered if their "scientific" approach, as they had called it, supposedly based on solid psychological research, was genuine. The bottom line, as far as Jacob was concerned, was that the seminar was a warning to all potential homosexuals, that it'd be best to satisfy normative expectations because non-homosexuals might want to hurt you otherwise. Indeed, he agreed with that.

But it's okay, he thought to himself. It was just a phase he was going through, probably excessive horniness brought on by hormones, and nothing else. He was normal. After all, those three guys went through the same kind of thing, and they kicked the habit. Eventually, like them, he too would become a *real* man.

A few months later, Jacob's father came home with shocking news. His company was retiring him. His father was a wealthy, successful man, yes, but also a geezer married to a trophy wife twenty years his junior; now that he'd turned sixty-five, they were giving him the boot. They gave him two weeks. Two weeks! A fortnight more of throwing his weight around as a big shot, then curtains. His ego was already fighting to maintain itself, slipping and sliding on illusory ground without any leverage.

Jacob hadn't been too affected by the news until he realized what it meant. The obnoxious tyrant was going to be home all the time. That was a horrifying thought. But it went from bad to worse when his Dad announced that the family would be moving out of state. His dad had decided he was going into the restaurant business with an old ex-colleague now living in a beautiful retirement community and golf club in a place called Dry Wells. Of course, Jacob's dad didn't know squat about the restaurant business, but that was the crazy decision he'd made. And this town called Dry Wells, Jacob had never even heard of it. He looked it up on microfiche at the school library, it was an obscure little place out in the southern desert near the border. It seemed insane to move from so-phisticated Seattle in the Pacific Northwest down to bumfuck nowheresville way down south. Sure, it might be fine for his dad who could shoot nine or eighteen holes a day sipping martinis, but what about his wife, who wasn't a golfer, or a senior citizen for that matter, and what about his children? What kind of social life could they expect there? Another reason his father gave for the move was that his restaurant-partner-to-be had told him that the dry weather was great for arthritis. Great for arthritis? Fuck you.

The move was going to happen in August. Only three months left of his time in Seattle, in the city he loved, the home he'd grown up in. It felt like he was awaiting a death sentence. Because one thing was certain, it was going to be death to his current way of life. If he weren't only fifteen he'd opt to stay behind, but that was impossible.

He'd tried having one of his conversations with god about it. About this lousy and unfortunate turn of events. He'd gotten very little in the way of a re-sponse. Wondered briefly if having to move was some sort of punishment because he hadn't really worked on course correcting his "abnormal" sexual urges yet. He couldn't tell if that thought in his head was his own or god's voice. It'd sounded different than usual, so he decided to ignore it all together.

Jacob tried not to dwell on it. He'd have to make the most of Seattle now, enjoy it to the fullest, take in as much of the city as he possibly could; hanging out with as many friends as time would allow. So he agreed when his friend Mikey invited him to go to the mall one Friday evening after school.

They met in front of the parking garage entrance as usual, grabbed a bite to eat and window shopped for a while before finally making their way up the emergency staircase to the top of the mall building. From there they had a rich view of the city at night; it sparkled in a cool, light mist. The air was robust; its redolence transported him to earlier childhood days.

Jacob and Mikey stood on the flat concrete top of the building taking everything in. Jacob would be leaving soon. The romanticism of it all was overwhelming; Jacob turned to Mikey and kissed him on the lips. To Jacob's surprise, Mikey didn't resist; didn't punch, kick, or call him a fag. Mikey reciprocated with a deeper kiss.

They hurried to the concrete awning by the door to the roof, their only shelter from the subtle drizzle. Quickly they cast off their clothes and explored the sensations of sex; the bed of cement didn't matter. They couldn't wait to orgasm, but were too excited. They rubbed against each other while kissing, felated each other simultaneously. Mikey bent over, spread his cheeks. Jacob lubricated Mikey's anus with a thick gob of spittle, and penetrated him. Though he thrust vigorously till the both of them lost steam, neither could orgasm; they resorted to rubbing against each other again while embracing and kissing. Jacob came first on Mikey's stomach. Mikey had to focus and masturbate to orgasm.

The fact of the matter was that Jacob didn't find Mikey attractive, not in the least. He had no intention of having a relationship with him, long term or otherwise. It was Seattle and all its possibilities that attracted him. Just the heat of the moment, as the saying goes. That moment being the beauty of the city as it resonated with his burgeoning youth. Apparently the feeling was mutual because Mikey hadn't said a word afterward; they both parted ways that night without speaking, and never saw each other again.

2
Inferno

Drought in the desert. Now that sounds like something normal, natural. Why of course, you say to yourself: the desert doesn't get much rainfall, so it's kinda redundant to speak of a drought in the desert — the desert is in a perpetual state of drought. Isn't that so? Well, it's a matter of perspective. Sure, when a river or a lake goes dry because of no rain, that's one thing. The desert doesn't suffer much from perpetual no-rain.

But even the desert has to live. There are critters out there, indigenous plants — and at one time there were even indigenous peoples — that do need some waterin'. That's just a fact of nature. Most living things go belly up in bone dry conditions. Not even Ezekiel can bring 'em back to life without moisture. Without Water. Well — puns intended — the town of Dry Wells is well named indeed, for it never had a levee, lake, river, or pond. Lately, not even a puddle. Natural puddle, natural bodies of water, that is.

'Cause there are puddles and pools in Dry Wells, sure enough, from artificial means necessary for human enjoyment and plain ol' survival. This kind of desert just ain't an environment meant for non-indigenous human beings. It's hostile to them, as it stands. It's a sand Antarctic. Not to mention that furious heat, especially in the summer. There's only one season out here, in general.

But going back to the idea of the desert drought: indeed, moisture is necessary, even for a desert. The desert thrives when there is rain, because it knows how to soak moisture up, retain it, use it sparingly, wisely. Patiently it waits for the next round of water to come, at which time it'll be sure to bank some more of the precious alchemical substance. The substance that transmutes to life.

So when a desert has a drought, now that's a drought. It turneth into a valley of dry bones, dem bones dem bones dem dry bones. And there is no reprieve from the heat, 'cause it's always hot even *without* a drought. Basically, it's an earthly preview of what it's like for evildoers postmortem.

But the good people of Dry Wells, Knobs County, didn't give a hoot about the drought. With the exception of the small liberal constituency, most believed that the weather was mighty beautiful — yet another sunny, gorgeous day, they'd say — and if crops, grown under artificial circumstances, were still suffering from the drought, why then the hand of god would have to be behind it. Now why would the hand of god be behind the dearth? Well certainly not because of the decent citizens of Dry Wells, the citizens who worship their lord every Sunday, paying god lip service whenever they can like the servile sycophants they willingly are. Of course not. It's because of the evildoers living among them. Those who don't belong. They do not belong in the world in general, because they bring the lord's anger upon the land wherever they sojourn and dwell, like Sodom and Gomorrah. If it weren't for good, Lot-like heterosexual Christians, those stamped with god's approval, why, every place the evildoers went would go up in smoke. There'd be pillars of salt everywhere.

Decent communities such as Dry Wells are well aware of the potential calamity-bringers among their ranks. Decent communities, for all intents and purposes, for the general welfare of their people, should set to weeding the evildoers out, spurn and cast them out. Patriotic citizens are obligated to keep a close lookout for all who would bring the lord's wrath upon the land. Public enemy number one on that list: sodomites. Homosexuals, that is. Look what happeneth unto Sodom and Gomorrah. Public enemies number two are (in no particular order): liberals, feminists, atheists, witches, bipeds of color other than that of the caucasoid, Jews, intellectuals. There are more sub-categories of the creeping bottom-feeder sub-species, but most decent folk were not prone to label with such discrimination. Why, they usually just lumped them all into one general and convenient rubric, say, 'undesirable,' 'abomination,' 'liberal,' 'fag,' and so on.

Dry Wells had been suffering a rainless dearth going on several long years now. Not even a darned sprinkle from a passin' twister. Just heat by day by scorchin' day, then — thank the lord — the cool of the desert night. At least they had that reprieve. Otherwise they'd be blastin' the air conditioner twenty-four seven.

But blastin' the cooler six, seven hours a day during the peak heatin' hours takes a toll on the pocket book. A big toll, in fact. So without a steady income, chances are a citizen could downright turn to jerky. And to have steady income, you gotta have a job. And if there ain't no job, why, that would spell unspeakable trouble, because nobody wants to turn into a crusty scrap of curly crisp. There is a double jeopardy here. Because if the income is low or non-existent, one cannot afford a cooler; food stamps and handouts won't buy electricity. Besides, food stamps and handouts are socialism. Socialism, again, is one of the evils that angereth the lord unto wreaking destruction upon the land. Hence decent, good citizens have to work and labor by the sweat of the brow in the lord's vineyard. Good citizens police other citizens, especially citizens who do not appear *normal* or Christian, to make sure they are not any kind of threat to their decent way of life. And of course, most heinous of all, they best pay careful attention so as to cast out the sodomites among them.

So yes. Sodomites — number one — then liberals, feminists, witches, atheists, bipeds of color, foreigners, abortionists, single mothers, and so on: these had to be watched-out-for, these had to be policed, weeded out, at least called out on. Why, back in the good old days, they'd be lynched, as would be pleasing unto the lord. The lord doth not suffer abominations to live, and forcing them into not living any more is but to work the hand of the lord on his almighty behalf. Doing good is not always easy. That's why it's called tough love. When the lord speaketh of love, he speaketh not of giving handouts to the lazy, of enabling evildoers to do their evil deeds upon the land. It's only natural to lock up and maybe execute violent, dangerous criminals. That goes without sayin'. But good citizens and good, god-fearin' folk understand something extra, namely, that god's law is a law of morality, and there is no difference between moral law and civil law. Why, moral law should become civil law. It should be enforced that way. Because when moral law ain't kept, that's when calamity befalleth upon a land. Hence, as some good Christians have learned, based on the research of some astute bible-based preachers, the lord's *testament* — which they knew was written originally in King James' English — was actually written in Greek at first, and the word for 'love' in it doesn't refer to mushy romantic sissy whimsy, but to *action*. So thou hast heard it said: love thy neighbor, that means take action upon thy neighbor, and that's all. Be proactive with thine neighbor. And that means makin' sure that he stayeth on the straight — so to speak — and narrow. And if not, well, it's time for tough love. Tough action. Time to exercise some muscle, as back in the olden days when heathens were slaughtered for worshippin' golden calves and what not. When fire and brimstone rained upon Sodom and Gomorrah because of fags.

Christian folk, the regular folk, most folk of Dry Wells had also been divided on the government during the monarchic rule of Ronald Reagan. The divide was reflective of their economic strata which crudely could be chopped in half: the haves and have-nots. The former believed Reagan to be the sign of hope for the future of 'merica. The latter believed him to be the Antichrist, the sign of impending Armageddon.

The desert drought. Granted, that almost sounds like plain ol' par for the course, but it ain't. Speaking of par for the course, there's a patch of green out there in the good town of Dry Wells, very damn near south of the border. You guessed it, the swatch on the landscape is a golf course, god's very own, owned by one of Knobs County's most prestigious Christian political families. But as to what they do, how they live their lives, ain't the business of anybody but them and their god. They have earned everything they got through plain ol' good ol' fashioned hard work, and the lord hath blessed them for it. As for the rest of the denizens, why, every non-Christian is suspect. But without digressin', the one golf course in Dry Wells is also a gated retirement community. A place for those who've paid their dues makin' the country great, to kick their feet up and enjoy the fruits of their labor. And shoot the occasional nine or eighteen holes, or more of course.

The shortage of water, the drying up of crops, and so on, drought sort of stuff, was of no concern to the geezers drivin' about in pink short sleeve shirts, checkered polyester pants, and shiny white golf shoes. Perfect golfin' weather. They talk about the dry heat, how it's good for them. Keeps arthritis at bay. All the while movin' from shade to shade, from one air-conditioned environment to another. Off in the distance not too far yonder is the bump on the flat landscape of Dry Wells, the small mountain called Knobs Hill. One time, ages ago now, the top of ol' Knobs Hill went up like a tinderbox because the mountain ranges way, way, way off in the distance — heck, over a good hundred miles away or thereabouts — were on fire. They'd been on fire for days, and finally, for some darned unknown reason, the top of Knobs Hill buckled from peer pressure. Why, it was the dry heat, the drought, you see. Everybody in the vicinity at night could see the reddish glow of the mountain fires on the horizon, and of course, they could also see the embers of the small mountain at night. Ashes fell all over town, smoke covered the sky; that is, ashes and smoke from the mountain ranges far away, mixed with some from Knobs Hill. Next day however, weatherman said, much to the delight of the pink-shirted fogies, that "tomorrow was yet going to be another beautiful sunny day." In fact, there had only been but one short break in the drought several years back, and darned if those geezers hadn't complained about the miserable weather, as they put it. It'd rained for about a day or so. No, just sorta drizzled, and the sky was whitish gray.

So the retirees enjoy the golf weather, the farmers of artificially sustained acreages despise it, liberals warn about it, and the rest of the good folks do stop and wonder why. Yes, why. Why *is* there a drought, a continuous, hot, infernal dearth of cloud and rain? Why not a mere sprinkle, even? It'd help if there was a canopy above the lord's firmament every now and agin. It would help with electricity bills for one. And if there was at least *some* rain, it'd shut the damn liberals up about a water shortage. More importantly, there wouldn't be an oppressive, looming sense of divine anger and disapproval. Little too close to fire and brimstone for comfort. Livin' in the desert is one thing, livin' in a desert during a drought is another thing altogether.

So there are at least two kinds of folks in Dry Wells. The well to do and the not so well to do. But in terms of being good citizens, why, there's plenty crossovers. And these crossovers? Well there's plenty kinds among them too, and plenty crossovers among those kinds. And so on it goes. Maybe when you keep slicin' 'em up into tinier societal slots like that, what you get are distinct individuals. That's true. But then again, the individuals have crossover characteristics about 'em. And that's what makes a society, which is composed of infra-societies. And individuals.

Well, there's these individuals in one of the infra-societies of Dry Wells, see, who call themselves desert rats. Just a designation that fell outta the ethers, who knows when, where, or how, or who said it first, all that's kinda irrelevant. Desert rats are just pretty much as they're called. Sorta dregs, riff raff, the undercurrent Rodentia of Dry Wells.

Sure, their kind exist beyond the boundaries of the town of Dry Wells, there ain't no mistakin' that. Desert rats are found pretty much everywhere where there's desert. They pretty much don't care about what kind of crossovers of society they entail, or embody; they actually pretty much don't give a shit about anything. Anything other than, say, partying. Biding the time. Finding ways to fill holes, holes that gather up to a streamline of hollow events in time.

They range from early teens to 'bout eighteen. That's the age spectrum. They get beyond that, they're real prison material, wind up either locked up or bumming at a street corner, or riding buses or cargo trains from one city to another, one state to another, aimlessly, lost, constantly talkin' to their own kind, commiseratin', constantly giving and giving till they got nothing left to give at all.

Desert rats mustn't be seen or heard. Again, because Dry Wells is divided, — and that division is clearly demarcated by the main highway that runs through it — as in the aforementioned bifurcation, namely, the well to do and not so well to do.

The main highway stretches west-east. To its north are the not so well to do. To its south are the well to do. And to its south is the grand golf course: Soaptree Country Club, a gated community of folks livin' high on the proverbial hog, and surroundin' that bastion of prosperity is yet another community doin' pretty much just as well, why, they just don't golf is all.

But because of the socioeconomic divide, those on the south side of the main highway, including the mayor himself and his family, are well cared for by a healthily funded police department that's on the lookout twenty-four seven, especially for undesirables, illegals, bums, and desert rats.

That's the strange predicament of the desert rat, and a desert rat is usually a male. The female of the desert rat species don't pose much of a threat; in fact they pose no threat whatsoever. However, the males are trouble. They got ragin' hormones, see. And they're usually fucking bored out of their skulls. So they're lookin' for trouble. That's why the cops are always on the lookout for them. That's how it works.

The strange thing is, desert rats come from *both* sides of the highway. And it doesn't matter which side the desert rat's from; a desert rat's a desert rat, there's only one kind, one specie, one genus, one taxon, and that there's about the size of it. If a cop spots one, the cop stops it. And when it's stopped, why, it's treated no differently from, say, an undesirable biped of color. And of course if a desert rat is also an undesirable like a biped of color, it'll be given shit all the time by the normative denizens. Like the undesirables, they simply aren't allowed to exist. So they have to hide, lurk, dodge the all seein' eye of the law.

A desert rat is usually stoned or high on somethin'. They're not big on booze unless it's a keg party somewhere out in the boondocks or on somebody's private property. Those parties don't happen too often, so desert rats don't do a whole lotta boozin'. No, they look for weed first and foremost. Next, they look for whatever else they can get their hands on. Acid, dust, coke, pharmaceuticals. Whatever. Last resort is booze, but that's the last resort, because even desert rats have standards. Boozin' just takes a 'em a little too close to bummin' from state to state, it's just too *hobo*. Weed is best. Then, whatever. Then, last resort, booze. That's the hierarchy of desert-rat values.

Jacob and his little brother Mitch had been forced to move to Dry Wells. Jacob kicking and screaming for the most part. His father had been a sales executive in the thriving metropolis of Seattle, a bigwig in his day. Worked for an old company that'd been around since the nineteen-thirties or some such ancient historical heritage. He was a company man who loved his company, and thought — no, firmly believed, as if it were his religion — his company loved him in return. But there's no unrequited love like a company man's love for his company, because companies are autonomous entities with a singular purpose; they're utterly amoral, they don't love you back. Not because they don't want to, they simply can't. They're like reptiles that way. Jacob's dad had been forced to retire. He got a pension, lifetime insurance and perks for himself and his wife, a platinum watch, a trophy, and a farewell by all concerned. He was out on his own, unready to retire, hoping against hope they'd see him as an exception, keep him around as a mentor for the upstarts; but the fact of the matter was he'd become a dinosaur. The company needed to shed its generational skin now and again, and especially with the times changing so rapidly, it had become imperative that he and his generation hit the road.

Jacob was fifteen years old, in the year of the lord nineteen eighty-six. Because of his father's decision to move to Soaptree Country Club, Dry Wells' retirement community, he had become demoted by sheer default — unbeknownst to him at first, — to the caste of desert rat.

3
Culture Shock

The August summer sky was bright. Very bright, like photophobia-inducing bright. Even the position of the sun indicated Jacob was no longer in the cool, Pacific Northwest. He imagined a giant magnifying glass in the sky focusing concentrated solar rays onto the one global spot called Dry Wells; he'd never before experienced such oppressive heat. Didn't matter that it was "dry," the way the arthritic geezers liked it, as they golf-carted from one palm-tree shaded area to the next or lounged indoors at the clubhouse sippin' cocktails.

Just look at those fuckers. Sitting in the air conditioned lap of luxury smack dab in the middle of the desert. Got all the water and lawn they need, made themselves an oasis out here. This place. This Dry Wells. Soaptree was gated. You had to have a code to get in and out of it, guarded by a rent-a-cop. The ever-so important little Napoleonic fellow, would sit in his little hut and watch his little TV. Every time his family'd driven through, he'd given Jacob a disapproving glare as if trying to will him out of existence so he could get back to his tiny TV.

The move to Dry Wells had been traumatic. Oceanic breeziness had been replaced with intensely hot stillness. Swirling clouds were supplanted by heliocentric tyranny. Hardly a soul swam in the community pool at Soaptree Country Club. Tourists did that swimmin' stuff, not the local retirees. Local retirees work on their swing, see, handicap and all that golf stuff. Where were the children of this community, the minors, the teens; they who would live in the future? Geezers and grownups everywhere. Yes. There'd indeed been a fall, a fall from metropolitan heights to a sandy land of artificially sustained decay. Jacob was on some kind of pilgrim's journey.

When evening would come and the sun started setting, the flat surface of the desert would turn fluorescent orange. Off in the distance — it was difficult to gauge just how far from his Soaptree home — was Knobs Hill, the one landmark, a small mountain shaped like a haystack. It was dark brown by day and would also turn reddish-purple-orange at dusk. The planetary atmosphere wasn't earthly; it was distinctively Martian. Indeed, Jacob had come to a remote, distant land far removed from his once familiar home, to an alien, forlorn, lonesome landscape.

After the family's first visit to their new church — their membership had been announced to the entire congregation during pre-service announcements — his dad's partner introduced them to the megachurch's Pastor Jim. He seemed like a friendly enough guy, hadn't given Jacob that look of disgust that all the zombies of Soaptree always gave him. Pastor Jim seemed genuinely interested in Jacob, and not in any creepy kind of way. It was as if Pastor Jim was curiously studying him, as if he were an alien from another planet. The first thing Pastor Jim said was:

"How'dya like Dry Wells, Jacob? Kindava change from Seattle, ain't it?"

Jacob smiled and nodded, didn't give him a verbal answer. Pastor Jim was still smiling, but there was some kind of slight — what the heck was it — micro-disapproval or something. It was weird. Jacob knew it'd be better to vocalize.

"It's very hot here," he smiled back.

Pastor Jim laughed. "That it is, yes sir, that it is. One of our elders is in the air conditioning business, you could say that was a wise career choice."

Everybody laughed. Mom, dad, Mitch, dad's geezer friend, and Pastor Jim. Pastor Jim's laugh was a hearty laugh that ended abruptly.

"'dja make any friends yet, Jacob?" He asked.

"No, not yet."

"Well, we have an outstanding youth ministry and excellent leaders. Go say hello. Jedrik is the leader of your age group." Pastor Jim looked around. "There he is. The lanky string bean with goggles."

Jacob turned to look where Pastor Jim had pointed, and sure enough there was a bone-thin dude just standing, not saying a word, in the church lobby. He was about six-foot-one or so, probably in his early twenties; his "goggles" as quaintly put by Pastor Jim were bug-eyes oval rims outdated by about a decade.

Scraggly, uncombed blond hair went over his ears and almost to his collar. He sported a cop-mustache, and his skin was pale.

This guy is the leader of my age group?

That was the first thought that crossed Jacob's mind. The guy was downright scary looking, something socially very removed, something extremely provincial and "small" about him. Jacob was afraid to approach him.

"Go on now," Pastor Jim urged him. "He ain't gonna bite 'cha."

Jacob thought better of responding with "we'll see about that," just nodded and carefully walked over to Jedrik the so-called the leader of his youth group.

He was staring off to nowhere. Jacob who came up to the level of Jedrik's shoulders, looked up at him. Jacob cleared his throat and said hi.

Snapping out of his reverie, Jedrik looked down at the unexpected greeter. Maybe he'd been contemplating what to have for lunch. Who knows.

He gave no response, so Jacob gave it another try, this time with more social ceremony:

"Hello. My name is Jacob, I'm new at the church. Pastor Jim said I should say hello and —"

"Mother Theresa's is down the street, boy."

Jacob involuntarily blinked a few times. "Excuse me?"

The skeletal specter's caterpillar mustache wriggled as he smirked and walked away.

Jacob, speechless, watched him exit the foyer and disappear out into the parking lot.

Mother Theresa's is down the street? What the fuck does that mean?

Jacob walked back to his family; Pastor Jim was gone.

"Did you say hi to him?" Jacob's dad's friend asked.

"Yes," Jacob nodded. "He wasn't very friendly."

He laughed. "He was probably hungry is all. Everybody here is friendly."

"And hungry," dad said. "Let's have lunch at the club."

That same Sunday evening after the second service, Jacob came back to the house feeling drained, too tired to shower even. But it was good to be back in the privacy of his own bedroom. Jacob's room was furnished with a brand new foldout sofa, desk, bookcase, and coffee table. His dad had decided to buy all new furniture; got rid of everything they had in Seattle, with just a few exceptions. Jacob's room was his one haven from the toxic environment outside. He was happy he had his own personal bathroom and shower just like back home in Seattle.

Home. He *was* home. This place, this environment was his new home. Still hadn't quite sunk in. It was too incredible. He'd been thoroughly uprooted from Seattle. His childhood home had been put on the market and snapped up instantly. Now there was nowhere to which he could return. When he would go back to Seattle — and who knows when that would ever be — he would be returning as a stranger, an out of towner. *Foxes have holes, and birds of the air have nests; but the Son of man hath not where to lay his head.* Ironically that had been one of the passages quoted by Pastor Jim during this morning's sermon.

And speaking of this morning, what the hell was with that Jedrik guy? Jacob was glad he hadn't run into him at the evening service, but oddly enough, wished that he had. He wanted to know what he'd meant by those strange, dissonant words. Was it because Jacob had dark brown hair, and slightly olive colored skin? Had Jedrik inferred that maybe he was a Mexican and a Catholic, and had come to the wrong church by mistake? Even so, what kind of uncivilized rube was he to greet him like that?

Unlike back home — back in Seattle, that is — the people of Dry Wells spoke with lilts and twangs; there was a tempo and rhythm to it, which lent even more to the sense of distant alienation. They seemed to speak a different language altogether. The people possessed an entirely different mindset, a stale culture, if it could even be called that, which seemed to exist in a static vortex outside of contemporary spacetime.

He replayed what had happened with that freak Jedrik after the first service; the brief encounter had left a tainted signature, a subtle pall that was still over him. Even just the memory of the experience had suddenly depleted him; leaving him without any kind of enthusiasm whatsoever.

But the fact of the matter was he'd have to attend church three times a week. Once Wednesday evening for bible study and short worship, twice Sunday for morning and evening services. Which meant he'd have to see Jedrik some time soon. He'd even have to interact with him, inasmuch as he was the youth ministry leader for kids Jacob's age—early to mid teens. Couldn't the church have found someone more appropriate, more personable? Maybe he'd risen through the ranks from youth ministry kid to eventual leader, by sheer default of seniority. Who knows, who cares. But it certainly wasn't because he had an amicable, approachable personality. So, since he'd have to connect with that Frankenstein monster of a leader some time or other down the line, he'd might as well try to get on his good side.

Jacob closed his eyes and drifted off on the sofa. Thoughts of sex with Mikey flooded his memory banks, but something was nagging at him. What was it? Some kind of conscience? He'd never given it any thought until the conversion therapy seminar, that his attraction to boys, masturbating and orgasming to the thought of boys, and having crushes on boys, was somehow unnatural. No, he'd heard the term 'abnormal' tossed around here and there, even 'aberration of nature.' What does nature do with aberrations? Nature rejects them, because nature enforces just what it is, itself, or *Her*self, whichever way it gets put, as it or She cannot be anything other than nature itself.

Was he indeed an anomaly, an abnormal aberration, or, as he'd heard Pastor Jim say in his sermon today, an abomination? And if he were these horrifying things, wouldn't god disapprove?

Jacob sat up on his sofa; thoughts of masturbation quickly subsided. He *did* believe in god. He *did* believe that he in his own humble way had a connection to god, even if an almost-conscious part of himself knew that the god he'd converse with was a facet of his own mind. It didn't matter. Maybe god was different from what he believed him to be. Maybe god was like a strict patriarch that rules with an iron fist; into corporal punishment, a spanker, a whipper, a punisher, a torturer, and a wager of war. What if? What if the god of Pastor Jim and Pastor Jim's church, even that ghost-fuck Jedrik's god, was the true god, and that he had been imagining that his own benevolent inner voice was god? What if he had been believing in an illusion? What if the situation was far worse than even that and he had been believing in the devil all along?

Jacob's stomach turned; he felt an upsurge of fear. Maybe he'd been wrong about a lot of things. Maybe his *joie de vivre* was just a byproduct of living in such a "secular" city as Seattle. Maybe his love of learning and reading was the devil's trick to throw him off the straight and narrow, one true way, his intelligence a hindrance because he was supposed to save his soul and believe without reserve, without thinking or asking questions. Maybe his love and appreciation of art, theatre, dance, and music were also the devil's ploys to thwart him from Jesus's bosom. Maybe his emotional, psychological, physical, sexual, chemical attraction to those of his same sex *was* simply downright evil, plain wrong, making him worthy of being stoned to death, worthy of divine wrath? What if? The thought-experiment made him feel nauseous; a rush of terror, white, hot terror flashed to the top of his head. *It can't be. Please tell me I'm not evil.*

But who would, who could tell him he wasn't evil? Could the god he'd known all this time, his friendly inner voice, comfort him now? Too late. He

could tell that that god had been ousted by the one
true god. The angry, muscular father in heaven with a
white beard, full of crazy commandments and demands from common sense ethics to animal meat
sacrifices to killing those who don't obey. Why
would the one true god ever tell people to kill people
especially since the first commandment is thou shalt
not kill?

No, don't ask. Just obey. Trust and obey.

Jacob fought back an upchuck and started singing
the hymn, tears streaming down his face:

> *When we walk with the Lord in the light of His
> Word,*
> *What a glory He sheds on our way!*
> *While we do His good will, He abides with us still,*
> *And with all who will trust and obey.*
> *Trust and obey, for there's no other way*
> *To be happy in Jesus, but to trust and obey.*
> *Not a shadow can rise, not a cloud in the skies,*
> *But His smile quickly drives it away;*
> *Not a doubt or a fear, not a sigh or a tear,*
> *Can abide while we trust and obey.*
> *Not a burden we bear, not a sorrow we share,*
> *But our toil He doth richly repay;*
> *Not a grief or a loss, not a frown or a cross,*
> *But is blessed if we trust and obey.*
> *But we never can prove the delights of His love*
> *Until all on the altar we lay;*
> *For the favor He shows, for the joy He bestows,*
> *Are for them who will trust and obey.*
> *Then in fellowship sweet we will sit at His feet,*
> *Or we'll walk by His side in the way;*
> *What He says we will do, where He sends we will*
> *go;*
> *Never fear, only trust and obey.*

He knew it by heart, he'd heard and sung it so
many times. The last line was especially effective in

soothing his fear: *Never fear, only trust and obey*. Because when you turn it around, what it says is that if
you *don't* trust and obey, then you've got something
to fear. And Jacob was afraid. Very, very afraid.

Jacob spent all day Monday and Tuesday in his
room. He only came out for lunch and dinner,
skipped breakfast. Reading and studying the bible
was all he did, immersed himself in learning god's
word. Maybe the fear he'd felt Sunday night was a
result of his not knowing enough about what the bible
had to say about god, and about Jesus. He searched
and searched, looked up the bible concordance for
passages containing the words 'fear,' 'sin,' 'punish,'
and so on. Some passages were somewhat comforting, some weren't, and both kinds seemed to annihi-
late each other, adding up to zero or negative-almost-
zero. The endeavor wasn't quite working out, but he
tried to reinforce in himself the command he'd always heard: *have faith*. That was about all he could
do.

He didn't masturbate either of those days, didn't
do it Sunday either. He didn't want to think of boys,
get aroused by them; he tried to be normal — as nature, no, as god intended — and think of girls, which
dampened his sexual desire. Which was fine. He
didn't want to be horny, not at this time anyway.
Things were just too confusing.

✦ ✦ ✦ ✦ ✦

Wednesday night short worship and bible study at the church. Though his dad had stayed home to drink and watch television, Jacob, his mother and brother attended. Jacob surmised that's how it was going to be from now on, that his dad would attend morning service on Sundays and not show up for the rest of the week. He was always about keeping up appearances. Maybe his mom too for all he knew. Mitch just tagged along.

When Jacob asked which bible class he should attend that Wednesday evening, one of the elders directed him to the room where his youth group met, out of the main auditorium, along the hall. Several classes were getting on in session as they walked by, each class chock full of about twenty or thirty youths. The elder smiled and opened the door for Jacob. Jacob thanked him went inside, took his seat in the back. About half the boys and girls — ages ranging between 15 and 16 — stared at the "new kid" in town, some of them with contempt. There was a total of about twenty-five or so of them in the classroom lit with overhead fluorescent lights. There were ten large folding tables clumped together in the middle of the room with chairs all around the square.

Though the kids in the room made Jacob feel unwelcome and more alienated than he'd already felt, he was more concerned about who was going to be leading the bible study; he wished, hoped beyond hope that it wasn't going to be that zombie fuck, Jedrik.

Jedrik moseyed in, bible in hand. He sat down unceremoniously at what seemed to be his designated spot, staring down the whole time. No cordiality, no personality, no joviality. Not a smile, not a greeting.

"Alright, let's get started," he said.

Jacob looked around at the kids; nobody seemed bothered by Jedrik, or scared of him like he was. Maybe Jedrik was O-K. Maybe he'd misinterpreted his strange words Sunday after church.

One of the boys spoke up. He was blond and somewhat skinny. Nice skin, smooth, no zits.

"Who's the visitor?" he said to Jedrik.

Everybody turned to Jacob; Jacob blushed. Jedrik glanced up for the first time and turned his goggled gaze toward him.

Jacob smiled, collected himself. "Hi, I'm Jacob. We moved here about a week ago."

Nobody said a word. The blond boy smiled at him though, and nodded.

"Where you from?" The blond boy asked.

"Seattle."

For whatever reason, Jacob's answer seemed to disturb the young Christians gathered in the room. Jacob couldn't get a read on Jedrik at all, who just sat there staring at him.

"How do you like it here?" The same blond boy asked.

"I like it," Jacob broke the ninth commandment.

"Do you miss Seattle?"

"I do," Jacob smiled at the boy. "I miss it a lot."

"What's Seattle like?" One of the girls asked.

"Gosh, it's a great city. The skyline is beautiful.

So much to do and see. There's something for every-one —"

And before he could finish, the same girl smirked and parroted Jacob with derision: "*Something for everyone.*"

But the blond boy quickly came to Jacob's rescue.

"It must be nice. I've never been, but would love to visit some day."

He smiled at Jacob; he wasn't bad looking. He made Jacob feel welcome.

"It's a liberal city," Jedrik said. "Teemin' with fags and undesirables."

Jacob blinked rapidly. He wasn't sure if he'd just heard what he thought he heard. All the kids were nodding and smiling. Except the blond boy, who was just smiling.

Fags? Undesirables? Jacob looked around the room. This can't be for real. And just what the hell did Jedrik mean by undesirables exactly?

"You ain't a fag, are ya?" One of the big, dullard looking boys said.

"Of course not," Jacob tried to smile at him. "No way, are you kidding?"

"Cuz if you are, I'll have to kick your ass," the oaf said. He had ignorance and hatred written all over his face.

"Or shoot'cha," Jedrik said, and grinned. Every-body laughed, except the blond boy.

Jacob laughed too, all the while hiding his shak-ing fingers under the table.

"'If a man also lie with mankind, as he lieth with a woman,'" Jedrik read from his bible, "'both of them have committed an abomination: they shall surely be put to death; their blood shall be upon them.' Leviticus twenty-thirteen."

Nobody spoke a word, just stared at Jedrik with glazed eyes, some mouths hanging half open. Jacob thought about bringing up the 'thou shalt not kill' bit but thought better of it, especially since the bible didn't seem to take that one too seriously anyway.

"Now who else's blood's upon 'em?" Jedrik asked.

"The Jews," one of the boys blurted.

"'at's right," Jedrik said. "'n accordin' to Leviticus twenty-thirteen, it says 'at the blood of fags is upon 'em 'cause they shall surely be put ta death."

The class nodded.

"Notice it don't say they *should* be put ta death. It says they shall *surely* be put to death."

They all nodded.

"'an that means fags and Jews should *surely* be put to death. 'at's what the lord is sayin'."

Jacob surveyed the room, feeling light headed like he might pass out cold at any minute. Everybody was gazing at Jedrik, their twenty-something leader, wise beyond his years, a paragon of Christian maturity.

"But," the blond boy said, "Leviticus says '*surely*,' does that mean we *have* to kill 'em?"

"Look here, Pat," Jedrik said to the blond boy. "That's the trouble with the liberal government and law. At least we got Christians in office now and they'll bring the lord's grace back to us. When liberalism's dead 'n gone, there won't be no more separation of church 'n state, see. An' that's how the lord wants it. How're we s'posed to obey his commands when we'll get arrested for it? Sure, we *should* by all means kill em', but it ain't worth gettin' jailed for puttin' a spinner in a lousy fag. Why, there's more fags than Christians. If every Christian killed a fag all Christians'd be in jail, see, and then who's gonna witness?"

The class nodded in silence at the wise logic of it. Jacob shot a glance at the blond boy — Pat as the freak had called him — and he wasn't nodding. He *was*, however, smiling mysteriously.

"But isn't that the old testament, the *testament* doesn't say we have to kill 'em, though," Pat said.

Jedrik smirked; his thick, ugly mustache twitched up and then down, once.

"Look here. It says in Romans one, twenty-six to twenty seven: 'For this cause God gave them up unto vile affections: for even their women did change the natural use into that which is against nature: And likewise also the men, leaving the natural use of the woman, burned in their lust one toward another; men with men working that which is unseemly, and receiving in themselves that recompense of their error which was meet.' What's that tell us?"

The class was silent. One of the smart boys spoke up: "It says they're gonna be receivin' themselves recompense meetin' for their error, an' that means they're gonna git what's comin' to 'em for doin' what's wrong."

"'at's right," Jedrik said. "'an whut've they got comin' to 'em?"

"Their blood is upon 'em," the burly bully boy said.

"'at's right, an' that can only mean one thing and one thing only, ain't that right?"

Everybody but Pat — and Jacob himself — nodded in smiling agreement.

"Galatians six, seven says: 'Do not be deceived: God cannot be mocked. A man reaps what he sows.' You sow faggetry, you're gonna reap what'cha got comin' to you, gonna pay for it with blood."

Jacob felt sweat trickling down his side from his armpit; he felt cold and clammy, yet sweaty hot at the same time. He felt light headed, his stomach was a conservatory of proverbial butterflies. The lunch he'd eaten earlier was rising halfway to his throat. He couldn't stop his hands from shaking.

"But didn't Jesus pay for their sins with *his* own blood?" One of the girls said, rather with a flat expression.

"Jesus paid for our sins, yes he did," Jedrik said. "But that don't give us license to go on sinnin', see. An' that there's the trouble with sodomites, they just ne'er learn. An' that's why the bible says they gonna get what's comin' to 'em."

Everybody but Pat and Jacob nodded. Why was Pat smiling? He made Jacob wonder. In this cold pit of social darkness, Pat seemed to be the one beacon of hope.

The rest of the session dragged on the same way about the evils of sodomy and sodomites, and about what an abomination homosexuality was with respect to both science and god. Jacob wondered what the hell that so-called bible study had been about. He'd been to hundreds of them before back home — or what once was home — and never before did kids and class leaders sit around discussing whether people should be killed or not. Sure, he'd heard those kinds of passages before, no mistaking that; it's just that they'd get glossed over, brushed under the rug; they would *never* be the core focus of any study, in any of myriads he'd ever attended.

He'd never felt so vulnerable before. How was he going to fit in with these people? Why did he feel so threatened? Why was he shaking? Because he was a sodomite, a fag? Was he? Did he deserve to get killed? Would they have mobbed him and lynched him if they thought he was a fag?

As far as Jacob was concerned, he wasn't a real fag. It was just a passing phase, that's all; he was just like everybody else.

Pat approached him after class; the rest of them ignored him completely. Jedrik of course said nothing to him, but disappeared into the crowded lobby.

"Hi, I'm Pat," he put out his hand to Jacob.

"Nice to meet you."

They shook hands. Pat still had the same smile that he had worn all throughout the bible study.

"Seattle, huh? Must be so nice there. I've only gone as far north as Iowa, if you can believe that. Seattle must be like, I dunno, a futuristic city compared to this place."

Jacob laughed. "I know. I wouldn't be here by choice, that's for sure. You lived here all your life?"

"No, thankfully. My dad retired so we moved here two years ago."

"Me too. I mean, my dad retired so we moved here."

"Where do you live?"

"The golf course, you know, Soaptree Country Club."

Pat's face lit up. No way. I live there too. Which street?"

"Chaparral."

"I can't believe this, I live on Chaparral too. What's your address?"

"73800."

"That's nuts. My house is 73801. We're right next to each other!"

After both families had introduced themselves as neighbors Pat rode home with his father, Jacob with his mother and brother. The two made plans to see each other again that night.

Back home his dad was drinking scotch and watching TV. He seemed to be in a good enough mood. Jacob quickly went to visit his new neighbor before that changed.

Pat opened the door with the same smile, invited Jacob in. Jacob said hello again to Pat's dad.

His room was a typical teen boy's room, quite a mess but a bastion nonetheless. Jacob discovered that Pat lived with his dad, and that his dad had gotten custody of him after the divorce for whatever reason. He also found out that Pat despised Dry Wells, just as much as he did.

"So, what did you think of our bible study to-night?" Pat asked.

Jacob shrugged, gave a subtle, exasperated snort. "I dunno. It made me nervous."

"Nervous? Why did it make you nervous?"

"You know. I dunno. I'm the new kid in town, you know how that is. I didn't feel very welcome."

"Oh, what Tracy said?"

"Who's Tracy?"

"You know, the girl that asked you about Seattle."

"*Her*. Right, that was so rude. What an idiot. Yeah, that wasn't cool at all, but there was also an overall hostility, like they didn't accept me. Especially that big guy, and Jedrik."

Pat nodded. "Yeah. You're right about them. Some of the people are okay, some aren't."

"Jedrik scares me."

"Me too," Pat stretched and yawned. "Man, I'm tired. Yeah, I feel sorry for little Josh, I can't imagine having Jedrik for a dad."

"Josh?"

"Jedrik's son. He's only four, he's in the toddler's bible class. He gets smacked around a lot by his dad."

"Geez," Jacob said, imagining Jedrik as a father. "I mean, that was the first bible study I've ever been to where people were talking about killing people. That was crazed."

"Yup. People talking about killing *fags*."

"And I've never been to a bible study that even used that word."

Pat nodded. "What do *you* think of fags?"

Jacob blushed. He was at a loss, struck dumb.

Pat laughed. "Stupid question. You're from a cultured background. Of course you're tolerant."

Jacob nodded and smiled. "Well, I don't even like to think of *tolerating* a particular group of people, I mean, who am *I* to *tolerate* them?"

"You're not a fag?"

"Huh?" Jacob blurted. "Wha-, what's that supposed to mean?"

"It means *this*."

Pat leaned forward and kissed Jacob on the lips. Jacob didn't resist; felt a tingle under his scrotum rise upward into his stomach.

Pat looked into Jacob's eyes, smiled, this time showing off his pearlies.

"But —" Jacob was speechless. "Are you testing me?"

"*Testing* you? For what?"

"To see if I'm a fag, so you could tell everybody."

"Gosh, you're paranoid," Pat chuckled. "I don't need to test you, I could just tell. "

Jacob stared back into Pat's blue eyes; Pat was being sincere. Jacob leaned forward and kissed him deeply.

"And let's stop using that word, I hate it," Pat said.

They laughed.

"You said you could tell. How could you tell?"

"I guess it's intuition. There's nothing overt about you, I mean you're not queeny or anything," Pat chuckled. "I could tell by the way you looked at me. I can't explain it, but you know what I mean."

Jacob didn't understand at all what Pat meant, but he nodded and hugged him; not wanting to over think it. How comforting it was to be embraced back, and how romantically cliche that they were mutual boys-next-door. Dry Wells might be somewhat tolerable now; they could have their own inside jokes during services and bible studies too.

"You — we — have to be really careful," Pat said. "They *will* try to hurt us if they ever find out."

They embraced, basking in the mutual warmth and relief of having found each other. Kissing, caressing, comforting, Jacob could have cried from the joy of it all. But the few minutes of bliss were interrupted abruptly by the baritone of Pat's dad out in the hallway announcing dinner; they swiftly broke their embrace.

On Friday while their folks were out to dinner with some other fogies and Mitch was at a sleepover — Mitch had fast become friends with the kids in his youth group, blended right in — Jacob and Pat had sex in Pat's room. TGIF as they say, not that Fridays mattered any more to Jacob's dad or anybody else at the Soaptree geriatric enterprise, but the end of the last day of the work week exuded the habitual sense of relief collectively, all around. The Soaptree Country Club Restaurant was a fine establishment situated in front of the driving range. In the evenings and into closing time it would sparkle and glisten in the distance away from Chaparral Avenue, as if it were a thriving citadel situated in the nocturne flatland, just a minuscule hint, as far as Jacob was concerned, of a simulacrum of Seattle at night.

They dove into each other's worlds, jumped in unabashed while their parents were out laughin' it up. Hungry, starved for affection, they absorbed warmth, took in smells of underarm deodorants, residual redolence of soap and shampoo, of fresh skin. Thoughts had gone blank, Dry Wells vanished. Home made its epiphany in the very immediate, visceral presence of Pat under him, above him, by his side. They simultaneously orgasmed on each other's stomach, absorbed in bliss.

Pat wiped their stomachs with tissues. He reached under his bed and pulled out a small cardboard box.

"I'm so glad we're neighbors," Pat laughed.

"Me too," Jacob laughed; they both laughed.

"Was that your first time?" Pat asked.

"No, actually. You're my second. My first was before I left Seattle."

"Oh. Do you miss him?"

"Actually, not one bit. It was just a heat of the moment thing."

"You're my second time too," Pat smiled, opening the box. "My first time was with a much older guy. He works at the country club restaurant."

"How long ago was that?"

"Believe it or not it was only a few months ago, about the time you left Seattle. Funny, huh? Like we were being prepped for each other."

Jacob laughed, then noticed Pat had pulled out a pipe with a large bowl.

"Is that pot?"

"Yeah," Pat said. "Let's go outside to the backyard."

The residual summer heat had cooled down; traces of deep blue and purple were still visible on the desert horizon. Past the swimming pool toward the back of the property was an ornate metallic bench; they sat there laughing and gossiping; on the same wavelength about the youth group. For one brief unpleasant moment the specter of Jedrik phased Jacob's memory. He reflexively shook it from his consciousness as if it were a pesky intrusive thought, the unwanted ideation getting attention merely for its sheer ghastliness.

Jacob noticed how casual Pat was with the unlit pot pipe in his mouth, talking away holding a box of matches; it was as if Pat was assuming Jacob was also a smoker. The matchsticks rattled in the box as Pat gesticulated.

"Um," Jacob interrupted. "I must confess I've never smoked weed."

"*Weed* being the key word, because you just smoked *me*."

They burst out laughing. Jacob was starting to feel almost punchy, that late-night sleepover feeling.

"Seriously, you've never smoked?" Pat handed Jacob the pipe. "I started smoking when I was thirteen."

"Wow. I guess that's what people do out here."

"Well," Pat paused. "There are two kinds of kids here. Church kids and desert rats. Desert rats are the scum of this society."

"*Desert rats*, huh? Are they like gangsters or something?"

"Nah, not at all. They're just burnouts that play arcade games all day and night, always on the lookout for the next high. There's nothing to do here, no concerts, no nothing. *Zip*. You're in a vortex now Jacob, the land that time forgot. Desert rats sometimes pretend and pose, but it doesn't last. Mostly just to score the next high. Everything else is futile and stupid to them."

"Are you a desert rat?" Jacob asked.

"You have to adapt," Pat smiled at Jacob. "I'm gay. I'm gay in a world where they'll kill you for it. Both desert rats and church kids will, because desert rats are just crossovers, they still think Jesus is cool."

Gay. The key word lit up like a neon sign in Jacob's mind.

Gay.

Pat was gay?

"W-wait a second," Jacob said. "Gay? You're gay?"

Pat laughed; it was almost a holler. "You are hysterical."

"No," Jacob shook his head. "I mean, I'm not gay, you're not gay either. We're just experimenting, that's all."

Pat paused, stared into Jacob's eyes. He sighed. "You disappoint me. Man, they really got to you, didn't they?"

"Who's *they*?"

"You know. *They.* Seriously? You don't think you're gay?"

Jacob fumbled for something intelligible, "I'm bi."

"Bi. Yup, I read that teens come out that way up north in the civilized world. When they *do* come out, that is. Ok, if you're bi you're bi."

"What I mean is, no, I'm not bi either, I'm normal, just experimenting."

"*Normal*? Wow. You are totally confused. Look what they've done to you."

"Whatever," Jacob scoffed. He didn't want to ruin it with Pat. "Are we going to smoke that or not?"

"Oh, yeah. You've never smoked, right? The first time is the best."

Pat held the pipe to Jacob's lips, scratched the match head on the crusty, sun-dried metal of the bench. Jacob huffed the pipe as the fire sparked the bowl. Jacob coughed and gasped out a cloud.

"You have to hold it in," Pat laughed. "Like this."

Pat showed him how; Jacob felt like a little kid. He made another attempt and successfully held the medium hit in for as long as he could till he coughed out the wisp of unabsorbed smoke.

"I don't feel anything," Jacob said. "I like the way it smells, though, like exotic incense."

"Exotic incense," Pat laughed. "Damn what a weird thing to say. You're pretty out there, in a good way."

"What do you mean?" Jacob smiled at the compliment while Pat packed another bowl.

"You know. Desert rats don't say things like that. They'll think you're a fag if you say something like that to them. Anything sophisticated or city-slicker is faggity. Fair warning."

"Oh geez," Jacob contemplated.

Pat lit another bowl for Jacob, the smoke of which he held for almost a minute this time.

"Are you sure this stuff works?" Jacob asked. "We're not just smoking Chinese herbs are we?"

"At forty bucks an eighth it *better* work," Pat said, smoking the rest of the bowl.

"*Forty bucks?* How much do you get for forty dollars?"

Pat showed him the small baggy. "A little more than this."

"Geez. I didn't know it was so expensive."

A drop in dimension, a momentary involution. Involuntary self-reflection and outward observation, mysterious dissociation. Spots emerged in vision, everything brightened up several notches. Tongue clung to roof of mouth, parched dry like the sands of Dry Wells. Bottoms of eyelids feeling swollen. Silent contemplation. Deep, deep contemplation into the not-so-distant past, memories from even five years ago were still somewhat fresh. But it all felt so hollow. *Hollow*. Without meaning.

Pat was poking the pipe at Jacob's lips; it took him a while to notice, to remember that he was sitting there in Pat's backyard, under the cool, star filled sky. Such pristine empyrean beauty above. Such a void, this town. Such a husk he had been, all this time. All was without meaning, had been so all this time. Only he hadn't noticed. Seems he'd noticed nothing at all up to this point, and now for the first time, he was stepping back and observing. An observer was observing. Never before had he fathomed there even was an observer.

When the observer was but a child, perhaps not even the age of seven or eight, he would gaze over the rail at Seattle's harbor, out toward the deep blue Pacific and think in his mind: *Squid, come. Octopus, come. Whale, come*. He would command them, as it were, monsters as he knew them to be, to emerge from the depths of the ocean, to rise to the surface. For he was confident they would hearken unto his imperatives and come. When he commanded the squid, he conceived of a being likened to the Kraken in size and magnitude. The same for the octopus. The whale, on the other hand, he thought of as a giant leviathan, a colossus of the oceanic depths. Perhaps an albino, without pigment. Its pupils would thus be red in color. The whale would be so enormous, the boy thought, that even its one single eye would be equivalent to the size of the planet Earth. Indeed, the whale was a cosmic fish, the concept of which he was unaware at the time. He only knew it was a very enormous whale. So enormous as to overwhelm utterly everything, even the sky itself. Seeing with the entirety of all of existence.

The boy was terrified of underwater creatures. No more horrifying a thought could there be than one of himself alone in the middle of the ocean, floating, open to the elements, with nothing but the incredible deep below with all its denizens. There were giant aquatic beings down there which rarely surfaced, if ever. They could be dinosaurs, prehistoric beings. They could be tentacled cephalopods, so large as to effortlessly take down an ocean liner, having the ability to travel at jet speed. With a single swallow they could devour ships, islands, the entire world. But being devoured was not frightening; their presence as such was the inherent horror.

He had a dream one night, a nightmare so terrible that he'd never forgotten it. He was afloat in the middle of a vast ocean, kicking with his feet to stay above water; it was night, pitch dark everywhere. The water was black; the sky was without moon or stars. Suddenly, the inside of the ocean was lit up as if a light switch had been flipped on. He saw all the creatures beneath his feet, brightly lit: the giant squid, giant octopus, the giant whale, and other giant inhabitants of the deep. They were enormous, and they were immediately beneath his kicking feet. So vivid was the terrifying sight, his consciousness swiftly thundered upward, out of the oceanic depths into waking space.

"I think it's working," Pat said, lighting another match for Jacob. "*Hello?*"

Jacob looked at the pipe, then at Pat. No words came to mind. No thoughts of what action to take. He didn't know the appropriate action for the moment.

Pat laughed, and lit the hit for himself before the match burned his fingers.

"I -," Jacob started, but could not remember what he was going to say. He couldn't remember it, something was on the tip of his tongue, ready to get vocalized, but it was gone. He tried chasing after it, but it was gone, vanished in a labyrinth of convoluted thoughts and memories.

"Want another hit?" Pat asked.

The question didn't register at first, it took him a while to understand it. The white whale with the giant eye, the Space Needle, the Pacific, the theaters, friends, acquaintances, the past. His father. How lost his father was. So immersed in nothing. Nothingness. Sheer meaningless nothingness. How could his dad be so stupid? A restaurant business partnership. What for? What was this place? Why did he have to move here?

Pat leaned in and kissed Jacob's neck, groping at his crotch. Jacob moved away from him, as by reflex. Pat's presence breached his inner and outer space, it was an imposition. It was too much to handle. He was getting nervous, he was floating now in zero gravity with nothing under him, nothing above him. Nothing but the vastness of the void. Nothing to grasp, nothing to stand on. No frame of reference. Maybe god was watching, maybe Jacob had lifted a veil he wasn't supposed to peer beyond. Beyond. He was glimpsing the *beyond*.

"I'm going to walk," Jacob squeezed out the words with herculean effort.

"Are you feeling paranoid?"

"Huh?" He wasn't sure, but the word rang a bell. Yes, it was quite descriptive of the overwhelming fear washing over him.

"Are you okay Jacob?"

Jacob took in a deep breath; it didn't help. Made him get even higher. Higher. High as a kite, as they say. Now he understood what that expression meant, first hand.

Pat chuckled. "Don't worry, Jacob, that's how it feels the first time. Enjoy it."

Enjoy it? Enjoy the sensation of freefalling in isotropic space, all the while introspecting about the hollowness and meaninglessness of existence hitherto, of his family, of his thoughts, of what he had thought of himself till now?

Jacob shook his head and forced himself to walk, to propel himself onward, shaking off the fear, the intrusive accusations within. One thing was for sure, he wasn't gay, no, that would get him killed. He was a reader, an artist of sorts, but that too felt empty and pointless. He believed in god. Yes, that was it! He believed in god. The still, quiet voice within. Maybe he could try to muster comprehending what god had to say, though he wasn't sure if he wanted to know. *Don't be afraid*, he said.

He made it out of the gate, didn't turn around to see if Pat was following him. Lot's wife turned around and turned into a pillar of salt. Forward march, onward, upwards, toward wellness, toward coming down from this terrifying high.

I'll never smoke again. I'll never smoke again. Please help me lord, I promise I'll never smoke again.

Chaparral Avenue had no streetlights. It was just pavement with houses on one side, a fence on the other partitioning off more golf course. Good thing it was dark, he wouldn't see anybody, and nobody would see him. He walked, forward, straight down Chaparral Avenue toward Highway 74. Crap he'd have to walk through the community gate. The rent a cop would be in his booth. No way he could put up with that. He turned on Ocotillo Avenue, same as Chaparral except there were big desert-motif houses on both sides of the paved road. No streetlights. How come they don't have streetlights? Streets were lit in Seattle. What is this place?

Walking made it better. He'd have to just keep walking, maybe he'd never come down from the high, but walking made it tolerable, kept thoughts at bay. No thoughts, no thoughts, please. Everything was scary, unpleasant, so hollow, so stupid. He was stupid, his life had been stupid, he wasn't who he had thought he was. It was a terrible revelation. Revelation. He only *thought* he'd liked boys, he actually didn't, no, how could he. Everything wasn't as hollow as it felt right now, couldn't be, simply couldn't. He had to be somebody, something, it all had to have some kind of meaning. He just didn't know what it was, but he'd have to learn.

Where are the answers? The bible, the lord's word, the word of god. Therein is the truth, therein are all the answers to life's problems, to life in general, therein is the knowledge of everything that there is to know, everything else is nothing. He had been too caught up, that's all, too caught up in the nothing of everything. It's a good thing he'd be going to church. There is nothing outside church. There's only pain, fear, and suffering. There is truth in the church. He needed truth, more than ever now. Pastor Jim, even that Jedrik as scary as he was, all brothers in the lord. Jedrik couldn't be all bad, how could he be? He was a Christian. He'd been saved, going to heaven. All Christians are going to heaven. All who believe that Jesus Christ is the son of the living god, amen, will go to heaven, as long as they aren't fags. Fags go to hell, Christians go to heaven.

I am a Christian, he muttered under his rapid breath as he paced onward. *Yes lord, I am a Christian, I am saved, I am not a fag, I will go to heaven, I am heaven bound, I will be alright, everything will be alright because I am a Christian who is saved because Jesus died for my sins.*

And thus spun his agitated wheels, induced by fear, until he gradually sensed the high reaching a plateau. He felt himself coming back into more comfortable, familiar sensations of existence. Yes, the high was beginning its downward descent and he with it. Descent, back down to earth from outer space and beyond, back down to where his feet could land. Back down, down, down. To Dry Wells.

4
Vision Quest

The much dreaded first day of school. The remainder of summer vacation had been tolerable. After that first high, the paranoia notwithstanding, Jacob looked forward to the next smoking session with Pat. In fact he wanted to score an eighth or a quarter or whatever of the stuff for himself. Sex with Pat while high was incredible. The experience was heightened; all five senses intensified coupled with an inflamed horniness he'd never experienced before. There were moments when the covert partners were utterly absorbed, without thought or worry. Thanks to Pat and pot, Dry Wells wasn't the unbearable hell it otherwise would have been. Church had been tolerable as well, maybe due to the THC that now lingered constantly in his system. It helped numb him from the vicissitudes of the psychological brutality and blackmail of bible study and the interminable politically oriented sermons. Even Jedrik was endurable, notwithstanding he was the same droning revenant that he always was, spouting righteous condemnations of all things unbiblical. Church sermons had been a routine snore for Jacob, ever since he could remember, even in Seattle; Pastor Jim's spunky personality aside, Jacob would lose interest as soon as he'd open his mouth to pontificate. He endured the otherwise tedious church time with fantasies of sex with Pat.

So all was fairly okay. Some adventurous avenues had opened up when Pat introduced him to a small gaggle of local desert rats — after sternly, repeatedly warning him to never, *ever* let on to anyone about anything that was sexually happening between them— with whom they'd shared pot and stories of delectable drugs they'd enjoyed. Jacob came to realize that drugs, video games, and heavy metal bands were all that these so-called desert rats talked about in their drawlin', twangy dialect, that they were, indeed in their own quaint way, bona fide connoisseurs and aficionados of all things pertaining to getting toasted. Sometimes they talked about *chicks*, but Jacob took the veracity of their conquest stories with a huge grain of proverbial salt. They were nice guys, pretty much. Uneducated, uncouth, uncultured, somewhat stupid, but okay overall. They seemed harmless enough as long as, of course, nothing *faggity* was ever mentioned. They were *cool*, which was their key buzzword — so to speak — a word that described anything they deemed laudable according to their peculiar standards.

Indeed things hadn't been bad, until now, the first day of school. He and Pat walked together at seven fucking thirty in the morning to the school bus stop on Highway 74. A few other kids who didn't live at Soaptree also caught the bus there. Their clothes and appearances said it all; they were from the lower socioeconomic strata, not necessarily desert rats per se, at least not the drug-devotee kind. Jacob wondered if there were girl desert rats. So far it seemed that the designation applied to dudes, to drugstore and convenient-store cowboys.

The rumbling, vibrating bus ride along the main highway toward the east end of Dry Wells was approximately thirty minutes long, with three stops along the way; loading more of the same kinds of cattle, speeding them all to their place of slaughter. The view outside the window made it seem as if the bus had been lumbering along on a treadmill, nothing but flat, insipid desert with spots of groves and homes from which the occasional boy or girl would emerge.

Public school. Now that was going to be something entirely new to Jacob. He'd only known his private Christian school with mostly white students, but the bus was already filled with Hispanic and black kids. Jacob was happy about the diversity, though he'd noticed that most of the kids kept to themselves. As if they were dead inside, had lost their souls unawares along the timelines of their vacuous lives in Dry Wells. Maybe there was a tension of sorts, but Jacob couldn't quite tell whether or not he was projecting his own onto the situation. Pat of course sat separately from him, pretending to be one of the commonplace, invisible children.

As soon as Jacob stepped foot on school property, an overwhelming sense of alienation came over him.

The school bell hadn't rung yet, some several hundred high-schoolers milled about hither and thither in front of the decrepit gymnasium. The school building looked like a cement prison; it had doors but no windows. Back in Seattle, every classroom had a window, so this was some ominous looking shit. It wasn't cool. School was a fucked up obligation, no, an ironclad requirement by *law*. Pat had told him about truants getting jailed, even their parents were getting jailed and fined for amounts they couldn't afford.

There was an ethnic diversity there, and a social one as well; as expected, Jacob could spot the cliques, the populars, the jocks, the geeks, the runts, the bullies, the stoners *aka* desert rats. Distinctions were blurry as there were crossovers, and at this point, he had no fucking idea which group he belonged in. He felt overdressed in his brand new button down shirt, jeans, and sneakers, though nobody, not even Pat, seemed to notice him at all. This suited him fine, until he was struck with the thunderbolt realization that he was going to spend the next three years in this hellhole without windows.

No, not today. Maybe tomorrow, but not today. He wasn't ready for this. He was still expecting the airy and well kept school buildings, playground, trees, fountain, and garden of the only kind of school he'd known. But this place. East Dry Wells High School, was like a fucking, run down gulag. He already felt like an alien on Mars in Dry Wells proper, and now this. He just couldn't do it.

The school buzzer rang loudly, a severe assault on the nerves. Everybody seemed to know where the hell they were supposed to go. Jacob had no idea. There were no informative signs posted anywhere. No supervising adults either, not that he'd want to approach one of them anyway.

As the grounds cleared, Jacob headed back out toward the main highway. He wished he had a joint. Even a lousy little one-hit bowl's worth of comfort. Because now he had a long, long walk back to Soaptree Country Club, back to his home, to his room, his one little haven. He couldn't wait to get back to the novel he'd been devouring, a turbid, cloying love story. He didn't care though because it took place in Seattle and it transported him.

The sky was without a cloud, and the temperature was already starting to rise. There was no paved sidewalk or walkway in sight. Jacob knew if he stayed on the main highway he'd eventually recognize the Hwy 74 turn-off to Soaptree. The directions were simple but the trek would be daunting, especially without any sidewalk. He'd have to stay off the paved highway, dodge the eyes of police cars, and look as inconspicuous as possible, evading the eyes of any do gooders. There was no desert in Seattle, no unpaved street of nothing but sand. He could walk literally for miles in any direction on sidewalks lined with shops, boutiques, restaurants, bars. No such luxury here.

This was the desert, the bona fide desert, literally, figuratively. With determination to return to his room at the house on Chaparral, even as alienating as the house and his family were, at least privacy awaited him in his room. It was his sanctuary and portal to his memories of Seattle. He would try to remember and savor every bit of the metropolitan mood he could get, like squeezing water from a dry cactus. Pot and his novel were waiting. His sofa, his own personal shower.

He walked as fast as he could, destination still distant, how distant he wasn't sure, but nowhere in sight. Toward the west was that one landmark, Knobs Hill. What a lonely bump on the desolate landscape.

A large Husky with white fur, black in areas, with two different colored eyes: one grayish blue, one white, materialized from nowhere, started following him at the outskirts of East Dry Wells. Jacob had no idea where the dog had come from, this canine he was sure, was not part of indigenous domestic wildlife. The husky kept a distance, several paces away, but tagged along *doggedly*, as it were.

Hours passed while he walked, very few cars swishing by. Not a single human being in sight, which was exactly what he had hoped for. He couldn't walk even a few steps in Seattle without encountering someone; here he had walked for miles in complete solitude, with the exception of the Husky, still trailing behind him. Jacob did't stop. There was nowhere *to* stop. No shelter, no shops, no cafe where he could walk in for a latte or iced tea, no place to sit and enjoy the ambiance. He was in an unsympathetic world, a forbidding environment, a sand tundra, the Sahara of the soul. He had no choice but to walk, to keep on walking, back to his room, his only tenuous refuge in the world, *from* the world. He had been uprooted and replanted in an arid soil roiling with innumerable "stickers," tiny entities like little balls of thorns, scattered everywhere throughout the land.

A couple yards away from the highway he saw a rusty metal rod stuck in the sand. Somebody, probably a desert rat, had rammed a crumpled hub cap through the top of it. It was a mockery; it took on symbolic proportions, cosmic, as if Dry Wells was sayin' *there ya go, ya faggit city boy, here's yer See-attle Space Needle, how'dya like me now?* He pictured the desert denizens laughing down at him from a non-existent vantage point, just everywhere, pervasive, hostile, provincial. Scary. He wanted to go kick the shameful totem down, the vulgar replica that jeered at him in silence, a pathetic, farcical parody that ridiculed his longings and wistfulness.

But fuck it, he had to keep going, no time to waste. He walked, kept on walking, away from the nightmarish mirage, on toward Soaptree. He was getting closer. The dog was still behind him. He began to feel an affinity for it, the Husky with two different colored eyes, male or female he was uncertain, who'd untiringly kept him company for hours now, all the way from East Dry Wells. Jacob was weary, sweating from the ever rising temperature; he imagined the dog must be equally tired, hungry, thirsty. Jacob had no idea the distance would be so great, the bus ride had taken only about thirty minutes. He was grateful to his faithful friend for having stayed behind him all the way. He was also mystified by the uncanny dog. He wondered if it was some kind of omen bearer, some kind of mysterious, spiritual sign. He had no frame of reference, means or knowledge with which to fathom it. So, he settled on the idea that the dog was expecting something from him, food most likely.

The Highway 74 sign was a welcome sight. School must almost be out by now. Didn't matter. He was glad he'd braved the unpaved sands paralleling the highway, rather than enduring that school, at least for today.

The Husky followed him to the front of the house on Chaparral Avenue. Jacob commanded the dog to wait outside. Quickly going to the kitchen — no one seemed to be home — he grabbed a few cuts of raw steak. The guardian with two different colored eyes was still outside. Jacob tossed the steaks on the ground. The Husky pounced on them, devoured them.

Exhausted, Jacob went to his room, stripped, showered. It was the first day of school, September of eighty-six. How could he possibly endure three more years of it? A year more, no, a month, a week, a day? What would happen now in this foreign desert land where he did not want to be, where he was utterly, completely forsaken, desolate, hollow, alone, in the middle of nowhere?

Pot helped. Pat agreed with his desert-rat friend George, who was somewhat of a marijuana evangelist in his own mind: pot is natural, god made nature, so god made pot, so pot is good. Yeah, that made sense to Jacob. So why was it illegal?

"It's illegal 'cause it lets ya kick back, see," George said. "They don't wantcha kickin' back and steppin' away from the crowd, see."

George lived with his withering alcoholic mother in a cheap apartment. George didn't go to church but was a believer just the same. Pat had introduced him to Jacob, and the three amigos would go to George's to get stoned after school. George had to sell drugs to support his lifestyle, but Pat and Jacob had some money saved up from chores. Jacob appreciated George's entrepreneurial pragmatism for the sake of his will to get high. Such things had never entered Jacob's mind, he was learning a hell of a lot of new sociological things. He'd been quite sheltered all his life, knew nothing about survival and drugs.

Indeed pot helped. Toke before school, after school, before bed, repeat. The directions worked. Jacob could make the best of Dry Wells with the help of weed and occasional sex with Pat. At night his father would go on drunken tirades directed toward him, his wallflower trophy wife, and sometimes Mitch. The boys' mother was powerless and useless in defending her kids. She had no comeback, nothing to say, took no action whatsoever. She took it all, par for the course, all the while oblivious to the anguish of her children — most particularly Jacob — as they were berated, belittled, verbally abused, psychologically pummeled, repeatedly, daily, for hours and hours till the wee hours, night after night. And the tyrannical, bored, drunken father would have sharp, discontinuous turns of emotion from hysterical, uncontrollable rage to giddy laughing jags. He'd make sappy, syrupy explanations of how his temper really wasn't all that bad; he was a nice, reasonable man. Which of course was a severe, obnoxious delusion. The harangues would last for hours, they were unending. He screamed like a madman; about Jacob's tardiness reports from school, about his constantly being out with his riff-raff friends, about what a dreamer,

bohemian, and no-good bum he was. The utterly insane alcohol fueled rage was incommensurate to its
object of attack in every instance.

The trouble was, Jacob's father was too bored.
The company stiff knew nothing else, had no appreciation for anything in the world at all except business, et alia. Ever since he'd been unexpectedly
booted from the company of his loyal devotion unto
whose altar he had sacrificed his soul, his scrawny
firstborn and dumb as nails wife were a pain in the
ass to have around. Mitch, however, was another
story, his golden child, malleable and uncomplicated.

Too much time on his hands; the restaurant business hadn't quite started yet, and even if it had, his
dad's heart wasn't in it because he knew diddly squat
about the racket. Booze was the fast track to altering
his ennui. Jacob thought the guy could use a good
dose of THC in some form or another and wished his
father would trying smoking weed. He knew this was
an impossibility. His father was an old school dinosaur, never questioned human conventions. With regard to marijuana he was an unflinching believer in
the *Reefer Madness* trajectory of hysteria and propaganda. Jacob wondered about the craziness of it all.
So-called reefer made you mellow and reflective,
which was illegal, and booze could turn you into a
fucking raving maniac, quite literally, possibly homicidal. It was all fucked up, everything was fucked up.
His father was fucked up, his school was fucked up,
his family was fucked up, Dry Wells was fucked up,
and yes, for that matter, church was fucked up. Fuck
Jedrik, fuck Pastor Jim, fuck the bullies and clones in
the fucking bible class. Fuck them all.

On one of the alcohol soaked nights of his father's rants, Jacob cut loose and told his father to shut the fuck up. It stopped his dad cold in his tracks, packed a punch alright, but what followed was an even colder, more calculated diatribe against Jacob. He dredged up and viciously articulated all the boy's quirks and foibles, dug at his soft vulnerable spots. Jacob's dam broke, all the pain from abuse he'd had heaped upon him ever since he could remember, came rippling up from the depths.

Hell, Jacob had learned — only recently, in an atypical fashion from his usually passive mother — that they'd taken him to a shrink when he was only seven years old. The little runt was a bundle of frayed nerves, always frightened, morose, worried, drawing pictures of kids getting tortured. According to his mother, he and his parents sat with the shrink while she asked a scared Jacob all kinds of questions. When the session was over the shrink asked to have a private word with his mother. She said the boy was normal, but that after having observed the father during the session, she realized that the source of Jacob's frazzled nerves was his father. The shrink boldly told Jacob's mother that her husband showed signs of clinical paranoia. She prescribed Jacob no medication but told them both — ever so circumspectly for the father's benefit —that they should never yell at the boy again. They must stop threatening him with loud voices because inducing fear was not a healthy way to discipline or raise a child. Even though his father later complained that the child psychologist was nothing but a quack, he stuck to the plan, keeping the yelling-at-Jacob thing toned down several notches.

Besides, back then, Jacob's dad had only been home after work and on weekends, unlike his current routine of loafing about, raising toasts to his glorious past achievements, twenty-four-fucking-seven.

So the dam had broken, ticking F-bombs exploding everywhere — it was just a matter of time — thereby altering the family dynamic— hitting an all time low. And the low was insurmountable. Like entropy, which Jacob had recently read about: the process was irreversible, headed for a deeper decline and more intense fucked-upedness. Mainly because nobody responsible was stepping up to be held accountable, nobody of character was rising to the occasion to fix things, make things better, do maintenance, upkeep. Jacob would sometimes try, because his father was busy throwing himself and everything else into a hellish maelstrom of sadness and anguish. His mother and brother were oblivious, thought their family was like any other red white and blue family. Jacob tried but it was futile, because his father was slowly committing suicide, unbeknownst himself, trying to preserve his ego by—literally and figuratively— drinking in the glories of the past to keep from drowning in the deluge of time. But after a while, Jacob just couldn't take it anymore, it was too damn depressing.

Pat told Jacob about a kid he'd known who'd found a legal way to get out of school without any hassle from the police. If there was any psychological hardship that made attending school difficult, and if Jacob were to be seen by a school approved psych counselor once a week — eventually once a month — he could do home study. Some kind of home study thing had been available all this time, who knew? He was going to do it, even if it meant having to put up with a fucking school counselor once a week.

But of course there were other logistical issues, the main one being — actually, the *only* one — his father. His father's permanent presence in the house, his sadistic prying, his rage, his drinking, his perpetually being on Jacob's case. He hadn't had to put up with his father while he was in school, but school had its own inherent ugliness.

There had to be a third way out of the dilemma. A few of the nightly fights had escalated to physical violence. Jacob and his father in a stalemate pushing match, his father punching him, Jacob doing a kung-fu-kick to his father's chest knocking him down. Too much insanity. Even his father wanted him out of the house. Jacob's mother and brother didn't seem to care either way.

Hence, one lucky day, when his father was feeling one of his manic highs, Jacob succeeded in convincing him to rent a studio apartment in West Dry Wells for him. He'd seen it listed in the Dry Wells Sun classifieds which he'd been checking regularly. An inexpensive little place where he could live separately from home. It was a stroke of good luck and fine timing; they drove, while his father was still sober, to the complex and rented the room. They kept it to themselves that the tenant would be a fifteen-year-old. His dad told the rental office clerk that he was renting it for himself as a personal office and library to use periodically. The story flew and thus began Jacob's private apartment life and psychological reprieve from home and school. He missed being next door to Pat, though. Oh yes, and fuck fucking church. He wouldn't have to attend any more to keep up appearances for the sake of his father, wouldn't have to listen to another bullshit sermon by Pastor Jim, wouldn't have to endure the righteous Christians in bible class as they railed against everything they deemed bashable, and he wouldn't have to see the ugly mug of that psycho Jedrik. Ever again. Fuck them all.

However, Jacob still felt the stirrings of a deeper connection with god, a deeper connection than his church would ever have allowed. It was as if his inner god was above and beyond the biblical god of war and vengeance. Was that even possible? All he'd ever been taught was that there was no god but the god of the bible, the god of the Reagan Republican Party, the god-the-father of our lord and savior Jesus Christ, the god under which the one nation of the United States of America had been built.

It had been reinforced year after year by the church directly, and also by osmosis, that imagination was something to be curbed, suppressed, and negated. Imagination was the devil's playground, it could take you outside of the safe walls of the bible and lead you astray. Imagination was something to be avoided if you knew what was good for your soul, because *all* is contained in the bible and anything beyond it is evil and of the devil. Nonetheless, Jacob imagined. He imagined that god intimately spoke to the depths of his being, knew exactly what was best for him and demanded nothing. At least it had always been that way.

He imagined the ancient land of Israel superimposed over the desert of Dry Wells, that it was no different here than it was back in the biblical days. He sort of bought into the Republican assertion that the U.S. had been founded on the bible, its god, and biblical principles. Didn't question it, just sort of enjoyed it. There was no moral principle involved in any of it for him, no ideological flag waving or patriotism, no, for Jacob it was sheerly about aesthetics.

It made the desolation of Dry Wells, its morbid lack of character, a little more tolerable. It added some dimension to it; particularly when he was stoned, he could feel it, absorb the very *mood* of it. Perhaps there was a mystery to uncover, maybe even some kind of epiphany. A vision, a fiery finger writing enigmas on the wall. He had heard of the Native American shamanic Vision Quest. Maybe that was something he must do. Now that he had the time, he could to do something like that, without getting grilled by his father, without the obligation of school or the oppression of church. He finally had some elbow room. It was an incredibly liberating feeling. Maybe a Vision Quest would give him an answer, a revelation, with regard to his mission in life. Maybe he'd have his burdensome homosexual curiosity lifted so that he could have proper desires like normal human beings his age. The getting-aroused-by-boys thing was starting to get to him; how much longer must his experimental phase go on? He'd had about enough of it, time for the normal, normalcy, normality. Sure he liked talking with girls, had no trouble at all with them, girls liked him. But they just didn't do it for him. He'd tried to think of them in a sexual way but that was a surefire way to stem his arousal. Boys were the default. At least in this current phase of experimentation.

Besides, there was terrifying talk about the spread of an ominous homosexual disease called AIDS. The media reports were calling it a gay epidemic, so having sex for curiosity's sake — and curiosity only, as it had always been — was now out of the question. Preachers were proclaiming it to be the scourge of god, punishment for the sodomites. No, he wanted no part of god's punishment just for having childish proclivities. The homosexual experimentation phase was now officially over.

And speaking of experimentation, George said he might be coming into some acid soon. That would definitely aid Jacob's Vision Quest. George always bragged about having tripped on acid for the first time when he was thirteen, though he said he'd known kids much younger than that turned on to the substance. And here was Jacob, sixteen and a half, having never tried anything hard yet. It was high time, so to speak, that he ventured into new horizons. George's account of little kids frying on acid saddened him somewhat, especially when he imagined their lost little souls flying high before their brains had had the time to fully develop. He understood why it happened though, here in this podunk, boring, scorching hot desert shithole called Dry Wells. He supposed all desert rats had similar fates, similar stories to tell about their upbringing, growing up without guidance, without education, all bible and church, without any idea of the world outside their unfortunate societal confines.

Jacob drove the used car his parents bought him after he got his driver's license, here there and freely anywhere. George lived in central Dry Wells about two miles away from Soaptree Country Club, on the other side of the main socioeconomic dividing line, namely, the main highway. There had been talk of building a shopping mall in town and a new main highway parallel to the current one thanks to the potential Reaganomics boom, but so far nothing had happened. Jacob relished the idea of a mall, anything that would bring a semblance of Seattle to Dry Wells. Wasn't holding his breath, though. He had pot, freedom, and the hope of a vision-quest adventure to come. That hope held more promise than anything the sad little hub called Dry Wells could ever offer.

George's dehydrated mother was plastered on the trash littered couch, as usual. The tiny apartment was depressing as hell, but George's room was the perfect desert-rat hangout. And it was there that George lifted up the baggie full of blue squares for Jacob to inspect and admire. He was charging ten bucks a hit for the so-called blue blotter acid. Jacob purchased a hit, being fairly warned to cut it in half.

Jacob would follow the doctor's orders. Back at his studio, without further ado, he clipped the mysterious piece of paper diagonally into a triangle, and popped into his mouth *right quick* as they'd say. He hoped it would prove to be an interesting night.

Dusk was fast approaching, almost six o'clock in the evening. Summer was near, the drought ridden days were unbearably hot but mercifully temperatures dropped as the sun went down. Jacob needed privacy from the world, and from other tenants of the complex, to be more specific. He drew the curtains, flipped on his used black and white tube, sat on the couch he'd moved from his room back at his ex-home, and waited.

And waited. Waited for something to start happening, but half an hour later, nothing was different. Unlike pot, there was no immediate buzz. He began wondering if it was "bunk." But George was a connoisseur with a reputation to uphold. He wouldn't sell blue pieces of placebo for ten bucks a piece, because somebody would kick his ass and he'd be out of business. George guaranteed him that it was fresh and potent, hot from some unknown chemist's lab. It might be cut with a little speed, George said, as was the case with most acid making the rounds these days. Pure "L" was hard to come by nowadays. It was a kind of drug Armageddon as far as drug pastor and philosopher George was concerned, the sign of the times.

Forty-five minutes, then an hour. Jacob had trouble focusing on the TV while he waited for the effects of the acid to kick in. He worried with each passing minute that maybe George had been wrong, that somehow, notwithstanding his sincerity the acid was no good. Maybe even the medicinal maestro had erred.

A tightness of the neck, a sensation of having to burp without having to burp. Weird. Jacob noticed he had been gritting his teeth involuntarily. Shadows began shifting along the walls as if they were being cast from the show on TV. Dreamlike fragments of recollections welled up in encapsulated Gestalts, perfect summations in singular bundles. He could see hieroglyphics emerging from the studio apartment's walls. They were so familiar, he almost knew how to read them if only they'd stop morphing. A mystical tome supernaturally penned in primordially cosmic scripts and enigmatic cryptograms had manifested on the walls, the ceiling, the floor. Spontaneous laughter; he couldn't stop laughing. Excitement rose from the center of his chest up to the top of his head and beyond. Swirls of colors, effervescent spots and forms danced. The tiny studio expanded into a courtyard, a grove of trees that spiraled upward out of the earth, a psychedelic sun shone above his head, illumining the hitherto invisible landscape. He could still see it when he'd close his eyes. Vivid, lucid. A bunch of smokestack piping, like from a giant factory came into view, horizontally laid on the ground. A large, black, metallic object with spikes on it, and then, his own portrait above it all, floating ensconced in the orange-tinged ethers. The world of dreaming had unfolded, a deep dream state while he was awake. He motioned with his hand, the swish left a slowly vanishing trail. He moved his arms repeatedly trying to observe the residues of matter and energy as they appeared in the spectra inaccessible to the day-to-day mundane mind. Millions of beings bustled in mitosis and amitosis on the TV screen. He saw himself falling in zero gravity, light as a feather, into the palms of giant hands. The palms cradled him like a precious baby whose eyes were closed, smiling.

Several hours after the peak, Jacob reflected on the fantastic inner adventure he'd had. He felt renewed, as if his soul had been bathed, washed in pristine light. He'd seen a mountain in the backdrop of his consciousness, majestic, under clear blue skies. The mountain trip had ended, leaving behind the satisfying sense of having dreamt without sleeping. He relished the afterglow of this most intriguing, mystical adventure.

Fortunately he still had the other Pythagorean wedge of the blue blotter. Feeling unusually energetic and content the following morning, Jacob decided to drive his *blowabout* up to the base of Knobs Hill. He parked on the dirt road and trekked up the trail used by hikers, dirt bikers, and four-by-fours.

As expected the trail was deserted save the indigenous critters: quails, the cartoon caricatured roadrunner, a hummingbird surveying a dry bush. After his virgin acid trip he thought maybe his "third eye" had opened up. A phenomenon he'd read about some time ago. Whatever the case, he felt like his soul had been cleansed of the muck he'd accumulated over the sixteen and a half years of his existence on the planet. In particular, the gunk of Dry Wells, everything about it, and even more specifically the psychic poison he'd been injected with at church. All that horseshit about fags, the subservience of women, the inferiority of non-whites, and so on. Yes indeed, the acid had proven to be an effective tool, facilitating the massive psychic dump that Jacob had so desperately needed. Goodbye church, Pastor Jim, Jedrik, yokels of the youth group and bible study.

Even the thought of Pat was unpleasant now, as if he'd been lumped in with all the other Dry Wells flotsam and jetsam. Made sense because Jacob was done with homosexual experimenting. Wanted to return to the state that god and nature had intended for him.

After all, sodomites were aberrations, despised in the bible, commanded to be put to death.

No, his personal god wasn't vindictive like that, but he'd still nag at Jacob's conscience, urging him to hurry up and get over the homo crap. Even at the conversion therapy seminar, although the Christian angle had been toned down, they'd been adamant about expressing how abnormal it was, how socially and societally unacceptable the behavior was. Jacob's homosexual activities must stem from a childhood remnant of some kind, the memory and excitement of the first time he'd discovered the pleasure of touching himself maybe. Must be some kind of empathy that he'd project onto another male, as if to say, *yes, I know exactly how you'll feel if I do this to you, so let's go for it*. That was probably the psychology behind it. His erudition was paying off, allaying his guilt, providing him with the scientific and psychological clues behind his homoerotic experimentations.

Jacob was done with Pat, didn't want to see the guy again. Wasn't in love with him, and luckily, Pat didn't love him either. No love lost. Pat was deluded anyway; confessing to be gay. He'd simply given in to his desire to continue experimenting. Homosexuality was nothing but an illusion. No, a delusion, a denial of the facts for the want of continued abnormal behavior, like an alcoholic who says they can stop drinking anytime all the while pounding a couple drinks a day. It was a perversion, plain and simple.

Now that he was sixteen-point-five, now that he'd been psychically cleansed, it was time to put away his childish proclivities. Time to go full on hetero.

Dry Wells girls were as uncultured and dull as their male counterparts, but Jacob thought there had to be at least one intelligent female for him somewhere in the damned dustbowl. He could pray for it. In fact, that's exactly what he'd do.

And pray for it he did up on the apex of Knobs Hill, overlooking the oblate plane of the sandy town below. Further off in the southeastern distance was a partial view of Soaptree's golf course. Before commencing the hour long hike to the top, he'd slipped the blue triangle between his cheek and gum like a hayseed clodhopper would a pinch of *tabacca*. It had come on rather quick — physical exertion must've sped the process — while he was still on the trail, en route to its zenith.

He'd never been to the top of the small mountain, let alone on the hiking path. Temperature was as high as ever below, nonetheless, the view, enhanced by the Vision Quest medicine, was astral. Without the acid it might've looked downright depressing, but now, he could again, with a deeper dimension, superimpose ancient Israel over it. The primal land of god's self-revelation unto the world. Yes, with the help of the acid, maybe Jacob would get taken up to god's empyrean paradise like Enoch and Elijah.

After all, he was a humble boy of strong faith, why shouldn't he hitch a ride on a fiery chariot? Or perhaps a personal theophany was imminent. He wouldn't mind if were. Colors and swishing trails pervaded the spectre of Dry Wells below. Even the brownish yellow of its ubiquitous desert sand shimmered with beauty. This is how ancient Israel must have been, this is how the prophets and Jesus must've felt.

Yes, Jacob felt one with them. Maybe he was being initiated. Initiated by god into prophethood.

5
Angry Gods

Jacob worked several odd jobs here and there. Even drove to Soaptree Country Club, avoiding his family's miserable home as often as he could, for his golf course maintenance crew job. It paid shitty minimum wage like all the other jobs he'd tried and quit — gas station attendant, car washer, restaurant dishwasher — but so far it was the most pleasant one.

Sometimes at work, when he'd see a shirtless worker ripped to the teeth, he'd feel that tingle in his scrotum. The girl-attraction thing wasn't quite happening yet, but at least he'd stayed away from Pat. He was just one of the guys now. He'd hang with a few of them after work and get stoned, shoot the shit 'bout this and that. They liked him and he was going to keep it that way. He'd managed to keep his homosexual fantasies at bay, though after a few days of abstaining from masturbating visions of shirtless and naked men danced in his head. He hated that, but hoped it'd just be a matter of time. He prayed for the ridiculous desire to pass, asked his god to help him become a real man like every other man.

In February of '88 a month after Jacob had turned seventeen, a PCP wave hit Dry Wells. Desert rats snorted, smoked, and shot the stuff. It'd take you to vivid cartoon land, distorting all dimensions and spatiality, giving you an immediate fry that would come on with a surprising rush. If purchased from the right source a small snort, about a match head's worth of the powder, could get you twisted for hours and hours. Desert rats would cut the stuff with protein powder, which preserved it, but gave it a suspicious brownish tinge.

Jacob blew his paycheck on a gram of the pure white stuff. He did it alone, kept his hard drug use under wraps from his buddies at work. Most of them smoked reefer but had a thing about psychedelics. All of them drank beer, and though he was still underage, he'd join them for a can or two after a hot day under the sun. There was camaraderie there, blue collar laborers, over half of them Mexican, making an honest living for themselves and their families; there was no racial tension amongst them, and Jacob liked that. He was kind of amazed, even, considering the social environment of Dry Wells proper. Even still, none of them, and he knew it for a fact, would ever tolerate a fag among them. Maybe the Mexican *vatos* wouldn't care as much, but not the other guys. 'Fag' was always on deck on the tips of their tongues, they used the word liberally without reserve while guffawing at each other's foibles and quirks.

And Jacob was no fag. He'd been suppressing his immature experimental tendencies just fine. For the most part anyway. At least compared to how he'd been. The early acid trips had been efficacious in making him feel prophetically divine, but they'd done little to eradicate the homosexual part of him which occasionally resurfaced. Acid did help, like pot helped make school more tolerable, but it hadn't taken his juvenile curiosity over the male body away. A few girls had made it clear they were interested in him but he was keeping himself holy, determined to stay a virgin until the right girl came along. The one who'd become his wife.

Yes, that was it. The right girl could cure him, turn him from the residues of his childish fantasies. That would have to wait, of course, but at least he had hope. And speaking of hope, he hoped that maybe this PCP stuff would initiate him into a new mode of being; to a feeling-like-Jesus mode and fully heterosexual.

Friday after work, home alone in his apartment with the baggie of dust. He showered off the day's grime, got straight to it. Fairly warned by George's supplier, Jacob took a minuscule portion — "about the size of a match head" — on the tip of a sharp knife, and snorted. Unlike coke, or *cola* as the desert rats called it, which he'd tried several times, the stuff had no exotic flavor, no numbing sensation. No waiting period like acid, even faster than weed, the stuff came on like gangbusters. The room and all its objects, brightened vividly with colors as if they'd been painted. Above all, there was the paradoxical sensation; an internal dissociation to his thoughts coupled with his feeling of oneness with a high power within. PCP was far more down to earth than acid, there was no paranoia either. He felt very in control of himself, his decisions, his faculties. He felt this way even though spatiality and time were gone. There was no telling how large or small the apartment was. The distance to the kitchen was impossible to gauge. He didn't know where the door was, so he couldn't go outside even if he'd wanted to. Everything seemed illustrated, painted by realistic and impressionistic artists alike. Dimensions beyond the present were accessible now, varying deeper states of consciousness, even the dream state. PCP created an altogether different modality than LSD and it was linked to his inner power.

The inner power, he realized, was holiness, the state of saints and the prophets of god; even better, it was a piece of god's bliss in heaven. He had at last reached the destination of his Vision Quest, a benediction, though ironically without any content to speak of other than the feeling of vindication about who he was, and why he had been born into this world. Indeed, he was a saint, a prophet.

Jacob was glad he had enough of the stuff to last him a while. He used it daily after work, sometimes even at work. He'd been on it even during the now once-every-three-months session with the school counselor. Nobody suspected a damn thing, although he'd blown some minds exhibiting an atypical self confidence. There was no way he'd been able to have "maintained," as the desert rats would say, in the presence of coworkers and others if the stuff had been anything like acid.

When his supply started getting low, Jacob cut it with protein powder. He'd been getting stoned often at and after work with a pretty cool co-worker named Tony. He wanted to try a snort of Jacob's PCP, even said he'd hook Jacob up with potential customers if he was interested in selling the stuff himself. Jacob needed a couple hundred fast if he were to purchase another gram of the uncut stuff, so, off he went with Tony, who'd vouch for the amazingness of the protein-cut stuff — he didn't know it'd been cut and it was still some powerful shit — to a bunch of older desert-rats sharing rent in a one bedroom home.

Temperatures had cooled to a nice seventy degrees Fahrenheit the evening he and Tony went to make their sale. As they approached the squalor, Jacob had a wistful pang, wishing for a moment he was back in his ex-home on Chaparral Avenue. He had indeed hailed from a different world, another economic stratum and tax bracket. George's house, the pads of other desert rats even, were decent in comparison to the drab, undecorated, utterly ratty shithole these losers lived in. They'd all been waiting there for Jacob and Tony to arrive with the stuff that would help them forget where they were, although it seemed they might not know the difference.

The dump was lit with a dim light bulb on a single lampstand without a shade, which illuminated the hovel in such a way that the shadows of the six fuck-ups sitting around the center dining table — yet another ratty piece of battered furniture, like their torn up and moldy looking couch — loomed and moved like nefarious phantoms. Grime, sand, crumbs, dirty shoe marks, garbage, and all kinds of shit covered the hideous, yellow-ochre 70's patterned carpet nearly bare from wear.

Jacob couldn't believe the six of them were living there. Tony seemed oblivious to the horrifying wretchedness of their abode.

"What's up dudes. We're open for business," Tony said. "This is Jake."

They glanced at Jacob, no concept of social ceremony registering on any of their faces. Though one of them lifted his chin in greeting. Not a smile, not a word. Jacob wondered if this was the way George was going to wind up, a destitute loser like these senior desert rats in their mid- twenties or so. Jacob certainly didn't want to end up like them, he could never do it. Shit, he was from Seattle, from a wealthy home, sheltered, from a cultured back-ground. And now he was seeing what rock bottom looked like, first hand. It was a sewer infested with sewer rats, lowlife low even by the poorest of Dry Wells standards.

"What's up," Jake said.

"I ain't buyin' till I try some," the spokesman for the brood said.

"Sure," Jake said, pulled out the stash to sell and tapped a tiny sampler onto a cracked square mirror on the table.

The spokesman had a case next to his elbow on the table. It was the most intact looking thing in the whole ramshackle sty; was about the size of an eye-glasses case. Out of it he pulled a syringe and spoon. Cotton balls were in the case too.

"Somebody get a fuckin' glass of water," the guy said.

With the delicate motion of a chemist the uncouth boor scooped the powder onto the teaspoon, using the tip of a murderous looking knife he'd had holstered to his belt. After he dripped a little water on the powder, one of the guys flicked a lighter under the spoon, moving it around. Spokesman placed a small piece of cotton on it, sucking the water up right quick. He set the spoon down, pushed the sleeve of his dirty tee shirt up over his shoulder. Another dude wrapped a tourniquet around his arm. Syringe in hand spokesman sucked up what he could from the dust-infused moistened cotton, then he proceeded to jab the needle into his vein.

Jacob saw his arms were bruised and filled with red holes that looked like hives; he started feeling queasy when the poison tester drew blood into the barrel. He quickly pressed on the plunge, and in it went, coursing through his polluted system.

Never before had Jacob seen anything like this. He was feeling as if he'd finally spiraled to the nadir of existence. The junkie closed his eyes tightly, furrowed his brows, turned his head up to the ceiling and began hyperventilating.

Was the fucker dying? Was Jacob guilty of homicide? The guy wouldn't stop hyperventilating, a whole minute that felt like it would never end.

"Yeah," he said, coming out of his indefinable situation. "It ain't bad. Had better but it'll do."

The others lit up with vile grins. Out of nowhere, each of them, with the exception of one, pulled out his own pristine syringe set. Jacob didn't care about getting paid anymore. He would've gladly donated the batch to them and dashed out the door. But he did need the cash, which they'd all managed to plunk down on the table: thirty bucks a line. Jake pocketed the money and poured five generous lines on the broken mirror.

With what Jacob guessed was enthusiasm, they repeated the procedure of the tester, nodding in approval as the dust ripped through their primate brains. The guy without his own syringe, the loser among losers, was given a shot with an old used one. When they were done shooting, they took the plunger out of their syringes and blew the trickle of their blood out of the barrel and onto the carpet. It was then that Jacob realized what some of the stains on the filthy carpet were.

A tall dude walked in the door. A woman — maybe in her late twenties or thirties or forties, it was impossible to tell — who looked disheveled, giddy, and wasted, makeup smeared, hair a bird's nest as if she had just taken a plunge in a vat of molasses, hung on his arm as if he were her hero. The tall dude, an even older variety of desert rat; about six-foot-six, maybe in his late thirties, oily, dirty blondish-brown hair down to his shoulders, scraggly beard, had also made his celebrity appearance to buy the stuff.

"Evenin' fuckers," the lumberjacky oaf said. The woman giggled.

Without further ado the giant took one of the used syringes laying on the table.

"Who got the stuff?" He looked at Tony.

"Jake, this is Roger. Roger, Jake."

What was Jake going to do, shake his hand?

No need, the hillbilly was like the rest of 'em, just stood there with bloodshot, intoxicated eyes that gazed off in stupidity. Jacob could smell the beer coming off him like a brewery.

Jake poured him a line on the mirror. Without payment, without a word the hulking rube did the junkie thing with spoon, cotton, and lighter, and without bothering to wrap the tourniquet, he jabbed the needle into his pockmarked vein.

Too drunk to gauge, he filled the entire barrel of the syringe with blood, then pressed hard on the plunger. The contents wouldn't go in.

"Fuck," the guy howled in idiotic laughter.

He pressed harder, but it just wasn't cuttin' it. Jacob was getting light headed, but he kept his composure. Under no circumstances would he allow himself to pass out on the infected carpet.

The clod jabbed himself in another spot, and this time the barrel emptied without a hitch.

"He's a Viking!" One of them said. The woman laughed. "He's my fuckin' Viking!"

A bedraggled, fucked up looking Viking. Viking weaved a little, still standing, wasted woman by his side, looking no different from when he'd walked through the decaying door. For a momentary blip Jacob understood why they cheered for him like a champ, at least the main reason: he was being extolled because he obviously wasn't a fag, because at least he, even the lowlife bottomfeeder that he was, was with *woman*.

Nobody, though, not even Tony, spoke on Jake's behalf about payment.

But Jacob didn't give a shit. He now had enough cash to buy himself the pure new batch and he wanted to get out of the diseased rat shack faster'n a bat out of hell.

"I want some," the woman said through a pathetic giggle.

Without asking for money, Jacob poured her a line.

"All right, guys, see ya," Tony lost no time in saying, he shot a somber glance at Jacob.

"See you, nice meeting --" Jacob stopped short with that and was the first out of the door.

Outside, notwithstanding it still being the lower economic dumpy end of central Dry Wells, was like heaven on earth in contrast to the interior of that ghastly pit. Taking in some deep, cooling breaths, Jacob no longer felt light headed. It was good to be out of there, that hellhole infested with sick demons. Never, he vowed to himself, would he ever, fucking *ever*, do that again.

Tony was quiet. He too was perturbed by what he'd just witnessed, which made Jacob glad that he, an amicable guy he worked with every day, wasn't one of *them*. He wasn't interested in knowing how Tony had come to know any of them in the first place. Connections were made in the desert rat world, but this one was the bottom of the barrel, so to speak. He'd known right away from Tony's glance that it was in their best interest to split the scene without charging the Viking ogre and his girlfriend. He might have pulled a gun, or threatened them with a knife the size of a fucking machete. It was just as well. The rest of them were too wasted to protest anyway, so Tony'd been right to cut and run, before one of the more astute dimwits could complain that they should all have been served *gratis* like Viking face and his distressed damsel. Yup, hit the road Jake and don't you come back no more.

Jacob scored his second batch successfully, augmenting the missing twenty from his own pocket. But he couldn't get the awful experience of having sold PCP to junkies out of his now guilty, lowlife-scum feeling conscience. Hadn't they heard of the new AIDS epidemic and that sharing needles could infect them? He could never jab a needle in his arm for a high, could never bring himself that low. There was a vibe of unwellness, sickness to it all. No, he'd never go that far, he had a better sense of self preservation. He was scared of AIDS, now more than ever, as if he might be smote for his having provided the substance that required needle sharing. When news of the epidemic spread like brushfire in '86 Jacob hadn't been all too concerned as it was reported to be a disease primarily affecting the gay community. Several gay celebrities had already died from having contracted it. They weren't sure if it was airborne at first, but Jacob surmised, in agreement with the few scientists who weighed in, that it was passed on by blood contact. Mikey hadn't had multiple partners and neither had Pat, so sex with them had most likely been safe.

Two weeks into his second gram, the inner voice of his personal god began to speak forth. He was wroth. *Thou hast fallen low to the company of scumbags, thou hast yet had sodomy on thine desirous mind; I demand atonement, a sacrifice. Thou must be cleansed of sin, for thou art my chosen prophet, and no prophet of mine is a homo junkie supplier.*

Never before had the voice of his inner god sounded like the god of the bible, stern, demanding something from him like when Abraham had to offer up Isaac.

Cold, lightning-white fear shot from his stomach up to the top of his head at the realization, after having come down from a dust-high, that god was putting his foot down, forcing him to do something drastic. He hadn't spared his only begotten son, that's how stern he was, so it would be no skin off god's nose to make Jacob offer himself up for sacrifice.

Sacrifice. It was a horrible sounding word, denoted untold pain and suffering. What would he have to do?

He'd been feeling deflated since the jaunt to the junkies lair. Even the wacky dust wasn't doing it for him anymore. He was burned out. And now this overwhelming angst, god's holy accusatory finger pointed at his very soul. Things were getting downright serious now. He just couldn't go on like this, still wanting to sew his oats with *dudes*, not to mention his having sustained his own quasi junkie-hood by selling junk to junkies. He'd never do it again, of course, just like he'd never *lie with another man*, but he'd already done the deeds. There was no taking them back. Now he'd been left with gut wrenching dread for the sullied state of his soul, for he'd lost his innocence somewhere along the way.

He hadn't been to church since he'd left home, he sure as hell — heck — didn't want to go moseying back there now to face Jedrik, the bible kids, Pastor

Jim, and Pat. He hated them all. Pat had some brains, but the rest were boorish morons. Plus, it had been a good while since he'd even cracked his bible open.

Best not open it now, not at this time. No doubt some condemnatory passage was going to pop out at him foretelling his doom. Doom, damnation, it was coming over him now, god's judgment for the evil little bastard he'd become.

And then, the holy voice within:

The sacrifice we requirest of thee, so thou shalt receive unto thineself purification to enter mine kingdom, thou must cut thine pecker off at its root.

No. Please god, no. I can't. I can't.

If thou cutteth it asunder, we shall forgive thee thine blunder.

No! Please god, my great god, please, anything else but that!

Jacob wept, got on his knees, struck his head on the studio carpet, prayed, supplicated, asked for mercy, implored that he be spared of the terrible sacrifice.

Take unto thee a sharp knife, nay, a gnarly scissor even, and get rid of the source of thine sin.

The inner voice of god insisted. Oh since when had that kindly voice of god turned so dreadful?

My lord god, I am not a sodomite, I have abstained from experimenting. I am healed of my childish foolishness, spare me the castration.

Alright, then, for cryin' out loud. Such a small price, would not thee payest for a ticket past the pearly gates? What's the big deal? But since thou art so attached unto thine cock, and art unwilling to offer it up unto us, thou art now on castration probation.

Yes! Yes! Thank you god. Thank you god.

But we still requireth a sign from thee of thy faithfulness. Thou hast been baptized when thou were a zit faced twerp, but now thou shalt receive unto thineself the true baptism.

What, god, is this baptism, pray tell?

Snort a goodly amount of dust, then go thou unto thine family's swimming pool, and drown thyself. Ye shall receive a sign from heaven, see, and thine soul shall rise, cleansed, unto our kingdom up 'ere.

But, but I don't want to drown myself, I'm scared.

Be not scared, for thou shalt be spared. Why, what's the big friggin' deal? It's just thine fleshly body, ain't it? Cast it off thee, be free, then thou canst join us. It's a hoot up here.

Jacob rose from the floor, poured the dust on his dining table, a large amount, about ten match head's worth, and snorted up every visible speck of it.

An intense fry came over him like a microfiche scrolling at the speed of light. He was sixty feet tall, then suddenly, the size of Tom Thumb. Morphing and bouncing from small to tall with each step, Jacob made his way to the car. Clouds were within reach, even though there weren't any above the droughty skies of Dry Wells. He was well accustomed to the fry, could even drive on it.

There was never any traffic on the main highway at this time. Past 9:00 pm the town always went belly up and croaked. The only signs of life along the way toward east Dry Wells were the heartstopper high-cholesterol dives, convenience stores, gas stations, drunkard bars and cowboy saloons entertaining their hicktown clientele till last call for alcohol. Not a single haven piping smoky, urbane jazz, where you could sit back and sip a latté. Coffee delights were a Seattle phenomenon anyway, at least while he had been living there; they had yet to make their way to this podunk charnel ground. Ah, Seattle. Bellevue, even Tacoma, shit, even Olympia. How he'd want to take a lungful of that Pacific Northwest air now, how the cities sparkled like Yuletide at night, three-hundred-sixty-five days a year. Skylines, malls, fine restaurants, men's wear shops, tranquil cafés, theaters, ballet, museums. If the Space Needle were here, he'd take the elevator straight up it now, and just stay there. Locals never went there, it was for the tourists, but oh how you just don't appreciate what'cha got till you don't got it no more.

Forlorn machinations bounced hither and yon in his cerebrum, all along the dead, lost highway. Sometimes his car would get jacked up high into the stratosphere, sometimes it'd get squatty like a flapjack. He was just a cartoon now, just a caricature of a human being, a comic book parody, a wasted husk, a sinner about to go drown himself in an effort to make things right with god.

Thanks to god's command that he take a hefty snort, he felt strong enough, no, powerful enough to see the drowning through. He'd heard about this kind of baptism once in a world religions class a long time ago. He'd liked the teacher too, a tall, handsome, articulate intellectual wearing wire rim glasses. Said there was a method of water baptism done in a river, somewhere in the Middle East, Jacob couldn't remember if it was a Christian baptism or not, but the baptizer would wait for the bapt-ee to say a confession, then they'd swiftly trip the bapt-ee by foot so he or she'd fall straight back into the water. The momentary shock of it would scare the pants of them, inducing a reflexive fear of drowning. At that very moment the bapt-ee's life would flash before their eyes. The teacher noted that by so doing, everything the person had done up to that frightening instant in life would have been reviewed and absolved, so that they could go on, reborn, ready to start anew.

Jacob had aced that class. It was in sixth grade. What an awesome, handsome teacher. No, never mind the handsome part. What an awesome teacher he was. Tall. Intelligent. Intelligence is sexy. No wonder nobody in Dry Wells is sexy.

He turned left on Highway 74, toward Soaptree Country Club. He couldn't take the employee entrance in the back at this hour, he'd have to go straight to the security gate. The guy in the window wasn't the guard that used to give him dirty looks. Maybe he'd quit, gone on to more verdant pastures. But since this guy didn't know Jacob from Esau, he'd have to talk to him and he was in no state of mind to talk to a rent a cop.

"Evenin'," the guard said.

"Hello. I'm here to visit my parents, they live on, uh —"

The guy sat in his booth just staring at Jacob. His visage transmogrified into a that of a demented hell minion.

"Um — crap, what was it."

Come on, Jacob, relax. Just a demoniac security guard, that's all. He pounded his head on the steering wheel.

"73800. They live on 73800 Chaparral Avenue."

"What's yer name?"

"Jacob."

"Never seen ya before. I'd buzz 'em if wudn't so late. I can't letcha in. Don'tcha know the code?"

Shit. Of course, the security code. Man he was fried. *Fried.*

"Duh, gee, how could I forget, it's been a while, so —"

Before bothering to finish explaining to the transmogrifying chimera, Jacob backed his car up to the security pad, punched in the usual code. The gate slid open: *entrez, le désert rat.*

Jacob nodded to the incubus, avoiding his face. Didn't want to see it. Didn't want the fear to get any worse than it already was.

A couple minutes' drive and he was there. All the lights were off. Good. That meant they were all asleep or watching TV in their respective rooms. It also meant his father wasn't on an alcoholic rampage. Otherwise he'd for sure be hearing the booms and crescendo's of his miasmic bellowing.

To his death now he goes. No goodbyes to his mundane family, for his heavenly father awaits him up 'ere above. Supposed to be a hoot.

The gate to the swimming pool was unlocked, no climbing needed. Standing by the edge of the water Jacob looked up at the star filled sky shimmering with confetti. No thoughts, just goin' in.

Jacob dove in the deep end feet first. *Amen halle- lujah* he thought as he saw an image of himself with a Nazi armband around his arm. Why that imagery popped into his head, he sort of had an idea. But down he went to the bottom, doing his darnedest to get water in his lungs. Gulp, gulp, gulp he did, swallowing gobs of chlorinated pool water till he surfaced, floated, gazing up 'ere to heaven.

"Help me father!" He yelled to god in heaven. Maybe a flying saucer would suddenly manifest out of the star filled sky. The top of the Seattle Space Needle would come hovering, yes, to send down a beam of rescue. Let it not be the top of the desert hub cap, please and thank you.

In spite of his effort, he hadn't drowned.

He'd had enough of the horror. Couldn't take it any more.

Maybe he could be forgiven now.

The living room light came on, his mother opened the sliding glass window. She must've heard his sputtering yelp to the ethers.

Jacob swam to the edge of the pool and got out, out of the suicidal scenario and into the kitchen.

"I'm home," he said to his mother. She had a puzzled look on her face, which was about the extent of her care. Didn't even offer to make him a sandwich just shuffled back to bed. And so ended the night of Jacob's suicide attempt. The inner voice of god was quieted for the night. He was sure that god most likely disapproved of his failed attempt at sacrifice. But, Jacob surmised, he'd been spared just the same. Like Abraham's sacrificing Issac, he too was stopped short of going all the way. He just had to show he was willing, and that was enough.

And boy was he glad.

＊ ＊ ＊ ＊ ＊

That same night, in the guest den, he got on his knees and apologized to god with much remorse, praying hard in silence to be forgiven for having failed to sink like a stone, for having come up for air. He also supplicated forgiveness for having refused god's command to castrate himself so that he might enter heaven.

But. But, he sayeth, prayeth, hardeth, that yea, he would not masturbate any more, never, ever again. That should compensate for his not having gone through with the gruesome alternative.

Indeed yes, that was his ticket to heaven. It had to be. He wouldn't fantasize anymore about boys and men, nor would he do the sinful deed of pleasuring himself; purposelessly spilling his precious seed by which he, like Noah was to propagate the human race.

And yea again, he would return to church, to the flock, as the prodigal that had gone astray like a dope, on dope. For he had had enough.

He slept like a rock that night, like a desiccated chunk of ancient desert sand fossilized, crystallized, petrified.

6
Jacob
and Janet

Everybody at church was surprised to see Jacob back. He learned that Pat and his dad had moved out of town, and that suited him just fine. No temptations, no bad influence. But the Frankenstein monster Jedrik was still there teachin' Wednesday bible study. The cast of characters hadn't changed much, they just looked a little older, some fatter. In particular, the potentially homicidal bully; he'd gotten wider, taller, and *thicker*.

It was awkward at first but he was prepared, psyched for it. Some were welcoming, which surprised him, some as cold and snide as before. But none of that mattered because he had a renewed determination to do right with god. He wasn't going to blow it this time, literally or figuratively.

There was a new girl in class, Janet. She had chestnut shoulder length hair and sky blue eyes. He could tell from her clothes, she was definitely from the lower economic end of Dry Wells. She was demure, shy. Smiled a lot, as if compensating for her inability to blurt out an answer, lucid or otherwise, to Jedrik's questions during bible study.

Since she was the new kid in town the heat was off Jacob's prodigality. He hadn't forgotten the alienating reception he'd received when he had been in her shoes once, ten thousand years ago.

Janet stood in the hall alone, probably waiting for her parent or parents to come out of the main auditorium where adult bible study was held.

Jacob didn't want the poor girl to feel the estrangement that he had once endured; he wasn't going to be a cliquish cold fuck who'd purposefully shun her, the new kid, because that was the tactic that was used here — most likely unconsciously — to make you want to belong, get accepted, be liked. Be approved.

"Hi Janet, I'm Jacob."

Janet smiled an enormous smile at him, just nodded, then looked away. Shy as shy could be.

"I'm sort of a new kid too. Sort of, I came here first in the summer of '86. I was gone for a good while, so it kind of feels like I'm new too, starting over."

Janet blushed, her ears on fire. She wasn't accustomed to the Jacob type. There were no others in this tumbleweed town who had the sophisticated flare that Jacob could conjure at will when needed. He'd learned to blend in, dropped his IQ points dozens of notches, said *fuggin' aye*, applied strategic twangs in the appropriate sentential places, all for the sake of his social survival. Standing out, especially here, could get you in a shitload of trouble.

Janet was endearing. She exuded a sweetness, which was a breath of fresh air here at Pastor Jim's church of rigid, righteous sheep. Maybe he should drop the charm a notch, he thought, but decided against it.

Janet. Maybe she was the one sent by god to cleanse him of his experimental homosexual leanings. Maybe she was the one who would cure him of his attraction to the male species, once and for frickin' all.

"Are your parents in bible study?" He asked.

She nodded, still beet red.

"I see. Where are you from?"

She shrugged, turned away, but still smiled, flushed from forehead to the base of her exposed neck.

"I'm from here," she said with a potent twang.

No wonder she was hesitant to speak, Jacob thought. But it was very cute.

"They said you were new here, today in bible study. Just new at this church?"

"Uh huh," she said. Janet turned away again, smiling, even redder in the face now.

"Well, it sure is nice meeting you, Janet."

She nodded, then managed her darnedest to squeeze out: "You too, Jacob."

You too, Jacob. She'd said his name.

"Um —" Now Jacob fumbled for words. But before he could ask for her phone number, out opened the door of the main auditorium. The adult group started filing out, gabbin', laughin', shakin' hands. Janet's parents must've been sitting in the back, maybe shy like their daughter, because they were one of the first to exit.

"How wuz yer first bible study young lady?" The dad approached.

"Fine," Janet answered, with a huge, *it was finer than I'd ever imagined it to be* grin.

"And who's this dandy young buck here?" The dad asked Jacob, lookin' straight at him.

"How do you do, my name is Jacob." He put out his hand. The dad gripped it hard, shook it. A sincere man to man shake. Jacob turned to the mom, who was also all smiles like her daughter. They appeared to be in their forties, father blue collar worker, mother stay-at-home housewife.

"How do you do ma'am, nice to meet you," he shook her hand also.

"*Well,*" the mom said, "such a polite young man. You ain't from around here, are yew?"

She was obviously quite perceptive. Jacob took off his desert rat sheeple cloak with them, and it showed like magical razzle dazzle. Made him feel powerful.

"I am originally from Seattle. My father, who is not here tonight," *too drunk,* "moved us here almost two years ago after he retired."

"Retired?" The father asked. "How old's yer paw?"

"He's sixty-seven, well, he will be turning sixty-seven in April. He was a late bloomer, I suppose."

Janet and her parents burst into laughter.

"But believe it or not I have a younger brother, younger by almost six years."

"Well ain't that sumthin'," the father said. "Sure's nice meetin' you, uh —"

"Jacob," Janet said.

"Jacob, yes, Jacob," the father smiled. There was a moment's contemplative silence.

"You wanna spend a little time here, Janet, with yer new friend?" The mother asked.

Janet looked away, then back at her mother. She nodded.

"Okay then," the father said. "don't be later'n nine."

"You must live close by," Jacob said.

"Walkin' distance, five minute or so. You two have a nice time," the father said, patting Jacob's shoulder.

Jacob was truly surprised. He must've created quite an impression on her folks, for them to so freely entrust him to be alone with their daughter. Then again this was church, there were plenty of folks around, so they must've figured it was safe.

"I will escort Janet back home, please don't worry," Jacob reassured them.

Thus began Jacob's relationship with Janet, who, amazingly enough, shared the same birthday as he, the exact same age to the day. It was kismet.

Her smile never waned every time they'd be together, in and out of church. It was as if he was her sun, and she couldn't get enough of baskin' in it. Jacob had no physical attraction to her at all, but felt sure he was working up to it. By all worldly standards she was quite pretty, cute. She had fully developed breasts, a grown woman ready to get hitched and bear babies now, by Dry Wells standards. There were plenty of young, very young married couples at church; their babies packed the nursery on Sunday mornings.

That was how it was done. Marriage between a man and a woman — be they sixteen or so and up — was also a mitigating expedient for expunging the sins of masturbation and premarital coitus. Thus, there was no disapproval whatsoever of those gittin' hitched right early. In fact it was commendable. For the married couple, regardless of age, were seen as paragons of purity. They were doin' what the lord designed for 'em to do, savin' the seeds for poppin' rug munchers and keeping the shared bed free of sin. And of course, if there were any of the *wicked* among 'em that would harbor lust for the same sex, why, marriage would solve the problem, set 'em on the path of righteousness, save 'em from destruction.

It was how Janet had initially reacted to his composure and way of talking, also how her parents first responded to his social decorum that had catalyzed in him a, hitherto dormant, self understanding. Yes it was those very moments that had sparked an idea in him. A magnificent idea. Downright brilliant. He had the charisma to pull it off, the charm, and sufficient biblical knowledge: he would become a preacher, a pulpit minister like Pastor Jim.

He got excited just thinking of it. He'd be a very, very, highly respected member of the Dry Wells community. The pervasive sheep, herd, and mob mentality of the population would get transmuted to reverence, admiration and obedience inasmuch as he'd emerge as their leader, shepherd, and moral exemplar. He'd have power, on a pedestal with a podium. Nobody would ever suspect him of having had experimental homosexual desires in the past, of having dabbled in drugs. Why, they'd come to him for counsel, spiritual advice. He could finally embody the message he'd received in those first Vision Quests; he was a modern day prophet of god. An upstanding man of righteousness, revered as the spokesman of god, an eschatological Christian luminary.

This could be it.

But, Jacob realized, single men didn't have the clout of the married man, not here, not in the Christian community of Dry Wells. A married man garnered immediate respect, no questions asked. A married pulpit minister, an epiphany in their midst. Of course Jacob was no sodomite, but this new path would absolutely put to rest any doubt on the subject, regardless of whether or not he had trifled here and there in the past.

Incredibly, Jacob kept his promise, hadn't spilled any seed yet, nor had he indulged in mano-a-mano fantasies since the night he earnestly prayed for forgiveness. Perhaps this was god's plan, the way to rid himself of childish homoerotic tendencies once and for all. Yes, he would come to fruition as husband, preacher and Prophet.

His new goal in sight, Jacob studied the bible, read commentaries borrowed from Pastor Jim's library at church, prayed, and even fasted. He designed his own personal training program. Janet was his spousal candidate. They went on plenty of dates, with the absolute approval and blessings of her parents. They must've married early too, like most couples of the demographic. It was the Christian, proper thing to do. And they knew, right out of the gate, that Jacob was the man for their little ol' Janet. After all, Jacob had continued to create quite the impression on them, with his wealthy upbringing, impeccable manners, and most importantly, his fervent Christian morality.

Jacob learned directly from Janet's father, as if by confession, that he and his wife *had been* alcoholics. One day they'd decided enough was enough, they turned to the lord and prayed for their deliverance. They abandoned the hooch and went back to church, which accounted for their absence at the time Jacob had first set foot on the holy ground of Pastor Jim's church. They too were prodigals, but Jacob felt no such need to share. He kept his former drug use — let alone homosexual experiments — under extremely tight wraps.

Janet's folks were kind and encouraging to him. They practically kicked up their heels when he mentioned his plan to enter the ministry. Why, they'd have a holy son-in-law, a man of god in their family. Janet's folks would have slapped rings on her and Jacob right there and then; declared them married if they could, till death do they part.

Jacob figured that was why they stopped asking the young newlyweds-to-be about what time he'd be bringing their darling daughter home after dates. There were no more jabs by the father about puttin' a spinner in 'im for untowardly touchin' 'is daughter.

That *was* what he and his wife wanted, now. For the young uns to start doin' some touchin' and feelin', and feelin' eventually guilty enough to exchange wedding vows before goin' full bore at each other. Wanted them to raise a family. That was how it was for most, if not all, of them.

Jacob saved up and bought a gold ring with a tiny diamond. He hid it in the trunk of his car along with a bouquet of roses. He'd made a reservation at Soaptree Country Club's fine dinin' establishment and informed her parents he was taking her out that night to the best restaurant in Dry Wells. Her folks must've suspected what was going to happen that evenin', so her mom took her shopping for the best dress 'n shoes her dad could afford, and a visit to the salon.

Admittedly, Janet was gorgeous that night. She smelled like heaven too. Jacob was natty in his suit and tie. The young couple turned heads when they walked into the restaurant. Janet couldn't stop smiling and blushing. She spoke very little, even tried curbin' her drawl, to sound more like Jacob. He thought that was quite adorable, notwithstanding how staccato and stilted it made her sound. After their meal, he got down on his knees— the waiter delivered the bouquet of roses on time—and proposed.

Janet said *YES!* with tears rollin' down her red cheeks. She jumped into Jacob's open arms while everybody clapped and cheered.

They subsequently drove back to Janet's home, and Jacob asked for her parents' blessings. Both of 'em in tears, they embraced the couple, congratulatin' 'em. The wedding would be arranged as soon as they'd completed the mandatory marriage training course at Pastor Jim's church.

Jacob dropped the news to his parents as well. Mitch was wowed, his mother looked worried, and his father told him he was a fucking fool. Jacob also informed them of his plan to enter the ministry, his father just laughed.

"All the years of my Christian upbringing have taken root, dad. It's what I want. I want to serve the lord and his church."

That sort of put the cork in his dad. He reflected for a moment, thought it over hard in his alcohol imbued brain, and miraculously said he understood.

Things were going Jacob's way.

The few days following the gloriously romantic evening, Janet was ablaze with sexual energy. Every make-out session at Jacob's studio apartment, or in Jacob's car, was intensifying even before their marriage training had begun. They'd gotten full on naked and explored each other, once. Janet's curiosity far exceeded Jacob's. She brought him to orgasm in her mouth, even drank his copious, pent up semen. He'd been masturbation free since he'd made his promise to god, so it didn't take much to make him climax. She came up with an enormous smile, gleeful. Happy. Jacob didn't feel any guilt for having spilled his seed because he was bound now to marry this girl. There was no sin, his promise to god hadn't been broken. He only wished he'd felt excited like she was.

Jacob couldn't bring himself to return her sexual enthusiasm and curiosity in kind. He couldn't understand it. During their intense foreplay on his bed, she had spread her legs open, hinting for him to enter her, or go down and explore the provenance of the human race. The musty, rather mushroomy scent of her wet, opened sex, repelled him. Her breasts were cumbersome obstructions to physical closeness and nothing more. In fact they were unbecoming. Her skin was too smooth. He momentarily gazed into her anus and thought of Mikey and Pat, trying to muster a little bit of desire. But he couldn't go down there, just *couldn't*. The whole landscape, not just of her sexual regions, was utterly alien. And repellent.

He struggled hard, very hard, to get hard, but all by the wrong means. Matters got worse, he started conjuring images of sex with Mikey and Pat, started replaying fantasies he'd had of other boys and men. Jacob was doing everything he could in his Christian power to cast out the demons from his head, fighting the good fight to stamp out conjurations of the male body and sex, pushing them down, down, down deep into the chthonic depths of his being, trying to reprogram his habits, his tastes, his foolish, childish preference for the same sex.

"We should wait till we're married."

He'd said it several times to her as she writhed all over him, as his way of staving off the eventually inevitable. That is, the eventual inevitability of his desiring her as a normal man would and should. The eventual inevitability of his maturity as a real, natural, heterosexual man.

It would take more practice. More sessions with Janet to get familiar with the female form, anatomy, scents.

Their conversations were almost non-existent. Janet was extremely shy in person, though she'd yack up a storm over the phone. It was strange. She'd turn her dial down to *mute*, and sometimes they'd watch television for hours without exchanging a monosyllabic word.

But when the makeouts and pettings would begin, she'd say uncharacteristically fierce things like *fuck me like there's no tomorrow, come on ram it in there* and such stuff that would perhaps make any *normal* man hot to trot. Jacob just wasn't there yet, although he was confident the time would definitely come for that. For sure.

"We should wait till we're married, Janet. I'm going to be a minister, you can understand. We can't have sex till we're married."

That was convincing enough for Janet, she wasn't devastated by the provisional rejection. She understood. She was going to be a preacher's wife after all. Though Janet's level of faith in god and Jesus was rather nebulous, having been raised a church brat, biblical matters were par for the course, just like with many of the kids at church. Few were actually fired up in the lord, as they would say.

And the ones that were, well, they were filled with righteous indignation against political liberalism, equal rights, sodomites, and so the list of the wickedness of the enemy would go on. Jacob was a little older and wiser now, perhaps he too must adopt those attitudes toward the enemy. He couldn't bring himself to go as far as Jedrik, talking freely about killing sodomites, but righteous indignation, sure. He was gettin' fired up.

"Well you two sure make a handsome couple," the youth minister and premarital counselor said. He had brown, curly hair, wore glasses and was probably Jedrik's age, mid twenties. He had a big gold band on his ring finger.

"I'm Ray by the way. We met a long time ago, don't know if ya remember." He put his hand out to Jacob. He shook his hand then Janet's.

"Sure, I remember," he lied, "Raymond, this is my fiancée, Janet."

"It ain't short for 'Raymond', it's short for Ray-bert. It's my middle name. You don't even wanna know my first name," he laughed. "Pleased to meet you Janet. Haven't never seen ya before. Have you attended any of our services?"

"Yes sir."

"Oh." He looked at Jacob, then back at Janet. "Are *you* a Christian?"

"Yes sir, I wuz raised in this church. I got baptized when I wuz thirteen, but my mom and dad ..."

Ray chuckled and shook his head. He adjusted his glasses, made a dramatic pause.

"I know 'bout yer mom and dad. But that don't mean you *too* had to stay away from church."

Janet looked at Jacob. She was at a loss. Though Ray knew about her folk's circumstances, he'd pulled a fast one.

"Janet was preoccupied and very sad during those tough couple years," Jacob came to the rescue. "But praise the lord, she's back, and so are her parents."

"Praise the lord, yes indeed, praise the lord she's back an they're back. And yew, Jacob. I heard yer attendance has been spotty too."

It hadn't been spotty, more like non-existent during the Vision Quest dust days of yore.

"Oh, yes, I live in west Dry Wells so I've been attending Dry Wells Community Church," he lied again. Hadn't stepped in a church once during the interim, except in good old Saint George's church of desert-rat delicacies.

"Well …" a look of slight disgust flashed on Ray's face. "That ain't a real church, see. They don't interpret the bible literally, talk 'bout symbols and what not. There ain't no symbols in the bible, see, just the facts, just the truth."

"Yes sir, I began realizing that, and soon as I did I came back here."

Ray sighed. "Well what took ya so long to realize? One service should've done it."

"Perhaps I just couldn't believe my own ears, like poking a sore tooth, so to speak. It was educational for me to experience the contrast, false teachings vs. the truth."

"Hm," he paused. "Yer mom and brother have been attendin', but'cher dad don't no more. Why's that?"

"He's unwell, sir. But he watches Pastor Jim's locally televised sermon every Sunday."

"Alright then. I hear you're fixin' to be a preacher."

"Yes sir I am. I'll be starting the ministry training with elder Jesse next week."

"That's mighty fine, Jacob. Mighty fine thing you're doin'."

Dramatic pause again.

"But'cha see Jacob, well, now don't take no offence cuz none's intended, but …"

"Yes?" Jacob could sense something more unpleasant coming.

"Yer skin's a little darker'n normal and you kinda talk funny. No offence now. But'cha look different, and sound … well, too smart fer yer age. Well, smart's fine an' good of course, you gotta have smarts to be a preacher. That ain't what I'm sayin', see. You know. You look and sound like yer frum outta town, like you ain't one of *us*."

Jacob was caught quite off guard, a bit nauseous.

"You ain't a Jew, are ya?" Ray grinned.

Jacob laughed a fake, nervous-as-hell laugh.

"I look and sound like a city slicker, I know. As for the tint of my skin, I assure you I'm a mix of German and Irish mostly, and my father has some southern France in him. That's where my sensitivity to the sun comes in. My skin tans easily, and I work maintenance at the Soaptree Country club golf course. I'm outdoors in the sun five days a week, sometimes six. The part about his day job was true, but Jacob made up the ancestral reason for his sensitivity to the sun. He really didn't know why he'd get tan but the rest of his family didn't. Maybe he was some kind of throwback, though he knew for obvious reasons that he hadn't been adopted.

Ray laughed a sincere laugh at that. "I like yer forthrightness, and thank you fer the explanation. I wuz just kiddin' 'bout the Jew part, I know yer parents ain't Jews."

He laughed again. Jacob and Janet followed suit.

"Phew. I know that wudn't easy to hear. I'm just repeatin' some of the concerns Pastor Jim and the elders had when elder Jesse told 'em 'bout the interview askin' for a ministry trainin' application you had with him. They don't mean harm, sure 'nuff they don't. They just want the church to relate to ya, and we don't relate too good to liberals and outsiders, if ya know what I mean."

"I see. I know full well, yes sir. And believe you me I ain't no lib'ral, nor am I an outsider."

Ray guffawed a hearty one at that.

"I'm sure you ain't, Jacob, I'm sure you ain't. And I know all of us don't think you are neither. It's just you kinda look n'sound like one, 'at's all. But'cher parents and brother look normal, I see the fam'ly resemblance too that you ain't adopted, and we got plenty white members that darken quicker'n others too. I jus' turn redder'n a *tomayta*," he laughed. "Anyhow I'll put a good word in for ya, Jacob. Everything'll work out just fine."

"Thank you sir. I really appreciate it."

"And stay outta the sun while yer at it," he laughed.

Jacob and Janet laughed too. Jacob would definitely have to quit the golf course job now.

"Well then, all that aside, let's git down to discussin' matters of marriage. Why do you two want ta get married?"

"Because we love each other," Jacob said. "We want to dedicate our lives to the lord and his church."

"You see, it's fine'n dandy to love each other, but you have to put the Lord first. Love the Lord first, love god first. Love your spouse next, your children next, when you have 'em. Do you love the lord your god and father of our lord and savior Jesus Christ, and put him before all else?"

"Yes, I do." Jacob said. He meant it.

"Janet? How 'bout you?"

"I do."

"Priorities. You two got 'em straight. Well, let me show you the six-session premarital counselin' program." Ray opened a drawer and tossed a brochure on the desk. *Premarital Counseling in Six Sessions*, it said up top, and on its front page was emblazoned a photo of a well-dressed white haired gent in white suit and tie showing off his pearly-whites. His doctoral credentials were listed on the same page.

"I'm excited about this," Jacob said.

"Yup. You can come in once a week, or if you'd like, we could up it to twice a week, Tuesdays and Thursdays. It's up to you. Today's the first session, so we got five left."

"We'll do the twice-a-week program Ray," Jacob said.

"That'll be fine. So here's the subjects we'll be coverin'." He opened the brochure and pointed. "First Session: The Purpose of Marriage. That there's our session today. Second Session: Preparin' fer Marriage. Third Session: The Laws of Marriage. Fourth Session: The Dangers of Marriage. Fifth Session:

Marriage and Parenthood. Sixth Session: The Perma-
nency of Marriage."

"I can't wait for the fourth session, *The Dangers
of Marriage*," Jacob laughed.

"Oh yes, that's a good one. A good lesson." Ray
said, lookin' at the brochure. He didn't get the humor.
"No *true* happiness is possible without Jesus, always
remember that. Sometimes, see, even married couples
ferget good morals and get led astray by improper
actions. But we'll cover that in the fourth session."

"I see," Jacob said. His mind wandered thinking
about what those improper actions could be. Oral and
anal sex?

"Now. The Purpose of Marriage. What *is* the reason for marriage?"

Janet looked at Jacob, who was facing Ray, and
back at Ray again.

"Jacob. Let's start with you. The husband-to-be.
The head of the household. What is the reason for
marriage?"

"To … have a family together. To bring up children in the word and morality."

"Okay. Okay. Good. Janet?"

"Yes sir," she swallowed, nervous. "To have a
fam'ly, to bring up children in the words and morality."

Ray laughed out loud.

"You'll make a fine wife, Janet, I kin see *that*.
You follow and are obedient to yer soon-ta-be husband. Now let's consider some of the *wrong* reasons
why Christians enter marriage. Number one: to have
lawful sex. Sex is a blessin' from god to be enjoyed
by married Christian couples, true. It ain't just for

procreation. True. *But*, if sex is the *only* reason fer gettin' married, then that's the wrong reason, see. Agreed?"

Jacob nodded, as did Janet.

"Let's see what the apostle Paul has to say 'bout this." Ray opened the bible and searched for the chapter and verse in question.

He continued the session in the same vein for an hour more, reading supporting quotations of scriptures. The young couple listened carefully to Ray and to the readings. Occasionally Janet would glance at Jacob to check his expression. He was poised, well-groomed, smiling, handsome, and occasionally nodding, occasionally whispering *amen*. When the first session was over, the couple stood up and shook the youth-minister-premarital-counselor Ray's hand.

7
Jacob's Wrestling Match

Ray must've kept his promise, puttin' in a good word for Jacob to the elders and hopefully Pastor Jim, because elder Jesse didn't bring up the skin tone and talkin'-funny stuff at all. He went right into the basics of pulpit preaching, handing Jacob a copy of an oldish book with a rather straightforward title: *Pulpit Ministry* by a well known preacher of the 1960's. Elder Jesse reinforced repeatedly that there 'ain't no symbols in the bible' that Jacob was to use *nuthin* but the King James Version, the *real* bible, the one and only true word of god uncontaminated by sneaky liberal propaganda like them other false versions.

Though Jacob had enough smarts — as Ray would say — to know that the bible was originally written in Classical Hebrew, some Aramaic, and Greek, he went along with it. Took it all in. After all, if that's what everybody believed, that god spoke in thees and thous, then amen, so be it.

Elder Jesse was rather polished, like Pastor Jim, and didn't use the N-word like everybody else — a word Jacob detested hearing from white folks, a word he himself never used thanks to his diversified Seattle upbringing — though elder Jesse did refer often to 'people of color'. He didn't use any racial epithets, and didn't use the word 'fag' either — like everybody else — but referred to those lost wicked souls as 'sodomites'. Elder Jesse went on about how the Jew was takin' over 'merica, however, and that it was always important to bear that in mind when spreadin' the word of god. After all, the church was the preserver of 'merican values, family values, capitalism, and morality; the bible was the foundation of 'merica, a Christian nation founded by Christian fathers. The Jew was an enemy of Christ and the 'merican way. Elder Jesse bolstered his statements, whippin' out the word and quotin' from the real bible:

"Titus one, ten through fourteen: 'For there are many unruly and vain talkers and deceivers, specially they of the circumcision: Whose mouths must be stopped, who subvert whole houses, teaching things which they ought not, for filthy lucre's sake. One of themselves, even a prophet of their own, said, the Cretians are alway liars, evil beasts, slow bellies. This witness is true. Wherefore rebuke them sharply, that they may be sound in the faith; Not giving heed to Jewish fables, and commandments of men, that turn from the truth.' Now what's that say to ya?"

Jacob pondered. "Hm. Yes, 'they of the circumcision' would probably refer to Jewish people, of the 'old faith' that no longer holds true, that their 'mouths must be stopped,' whatever that means."

"*Whatever that means?*" Elder Jesse sighed in exasperation. "That ain't gonna do, son. You're the preacher now, think like a preacher. You cain't get up 'ere on the pulpit and say, 'whatever that means,' now can ya? You gotta teach, son, *teach*. The church is listenin' and hangin' on yer every word. So let's try that agin. What's that say to ya?"

Jacob chuckled nervously. "Yes sir, I'm sorry. You're right. Well, the passage says that they must be rebuked sharply, so that they may be sound in the faith. Which, well, almost seems to imply that the Jewish people referred to in the passage are Christian converts."

Elder Jesse read the passage over in silence. He didn't say anything.

"Let's try the next one, then, first Thessalonians, two, fourteen ta sixteen: 'For ye, brethren, became followers of the churches of God which in Judaea are in Christ Jesus: for ye also have suffered like things of your own countrymen, even as they have of the Jews: Who both killed the Lord Jesus, and their own prophets, and have persecuted us; and they please not God, and are contrary to all men: Forbidding us to speak to the Gentiles that they might be saved, to fill up their sins alway: for the wrath is come upon them to the uttermost.' What's 'at tell ya?"

Jacob wasn't sure where this was headed. He wanted to be a preacher, not a radical anti-semite. The passage, which of course was the absolute word of god, says straight out that the Jews killed lord Jesus, that the Jewish people killed their own prophets and have persecuted Christians, that they aren't pleasing to god, and that they are contrary to all men. Thus, in conclusion, uttermost wrath has come upon them, *whatever that means.*

"Yes. Yes, the Jewish people are definitely denounced here, very true."

"They're enemies of the Lord Jesus. They're enemies of Christians. They're enemies of all men. Ain't that so? Didn't the uttermost wrath come upon them? Wudn't the Holocaust justified? Why, they killed Jesus!"

He'd never thought of it that way. Still couldn't think, no matter how hated the Jewish people are and were by Christians, that the Holocaust was justifiable. That was outright fucking — frigging — psychotic. Jacob clammed up, not knowing what to say, and as elder Jesse said, that wouldn't do. What if he, for whatever reason, had to read this passage from the pulpit? Then what? How was he going to give an explanation of it?

"Well, sir, I think it's quite straightforward."

"Darn right it's quite straightforward. And mind you, don't use five-dollar words like 'at, like 'straightforward'. You gotta crank it down a few notches, see, so the church members kin understand ya. That's an important thing you gotta always remember, Jacob. You're obviously a very intelligent young man. People git scared of people like you. So you gotta relate to 'em at their level, where they feel comfortable, you gotta become like *them*, see, talk like 'em and think like 'em."

"Yes sir. I understand. That makes a lot of sense."

"Good. Preachin's a lot harder'n you thought, huh? There's more to it than going up 'ere and givin' a lecture. You gotta understand *people*. You could be a highfalutin' biblical scholar and professor, but that don't mean squat, see. You gotta speak at the people's level, and that there, Jacob, is something I'll keep stressin' till the cows come home."

"Yes sir."

"Yer polite, intelligent, and good lookin' ... don't get me wrong on that last one," elder Jim laughed.

Jacob smiled at him and shook his head.

"You got all the goods to make a fine preacher. The only thing you gotta work on is tonin' down yer vocabulary and intelligence. Sounds kinda funny, I know, but that's the only way you can relate to members. *All* members equally."

"Understood. Thank you sir, elder Jesse, for the kind compliments."

"Well yer very welcome, Jacob. Very welcome."

And so on it went, with some feminism, abortion, and lesbian issues thrown in for good measure. After the biblical interpretation and exegesis lesson, elder Jesse briefly touched on the subject of public speaking, a subject that would be covered at length in the next training session. At the end of the three-times-a-week, three month program Jacob would be given an oral exam on his knowledge of biblical passages, which he'd have to know by chapter and verse. He'd have to have a lot of key passages memorized as well. For the final exam he'd be required to give a sermon to the panel of elders, deacons, and Pastor Jim. They'd evaluate the sermon and based on his performance they'd either give him the green light or nix his future career.

Jacob and Janet were hitched a week after the mandatory marriage counseling sessions were completed. The big event was held in the church auditorium after morning service. The party *sans* booze, music, and dancing — just a buffet, a healthy spread at that, with wedding cake, sodas, coffee, all out of Jacob's dad's pocket — was held outside on the picnic grounds. Jacob's dad had also hired uniformed staff from the Soaptree restaurant to wait on the new couple and their families, Pastor Jim and the elders, and the twelve attendants of honor. Most of the members present at the morning service attended, at least five hundred folks of all ages. Pastor Jim presided over the wedding vows and official declaration of *man and wife*. The sealing kiss was a quick, shy peck on the lips, no tongue-down-the-throat high drama.

Janet was an ethereal sight in her wedding dress. Must've cost her folks a hefty sum. Matching bridesmaids's dresses, six of them, were rented. Jacob was in a light blue tux, and his entourage of six men including the strategically chosen Jedrik as best man, were in matching tuxes as well, all rented, of course. Jacob was grateful to his father for what he had done; he was on his best behavior at the party too, wasn't soused in the least. Jedrik's speech as best man was short and dry: "Jake here's gonna make a fine husband, and if all ya don't know yet, he's fixin' to be a preacher and overseer of the youth ministry. I'm gonna have a new boss" — at which everybody laughed — "I'm impressed at how Jake's grown in the lord, and I wish him and his new wife the best, that they put god first and serve the lord and his church."

Jedrik's six year old son Josh had also been fitted in a small tux. The boy typically never smiled, always looked pensive and morose, but at the party he was scurryin' about havin' fun with all the other rugrats. Jacob was glad to see that, as he'd always been concerned about the boy since he'd heard the rumors about his dad smackin' and beatin' him. Never mind the fact that his father was an outspoken fag-basher and racist on top of it all.

All in all it was a glorious day. Jacob's father had rented the couple a chauffeured limo from the Country Club, all packed with honeymoon luggage, which was a surprise he'd chosen not to reveal till it showed up. The newlyweds got whisked off, partygoers cheerin', hootin', and wavin' at 'em as they drove off into the sunset, toward the best hotel several miles north of Dry Wells proper, a good hour's drive. They were to spend their wedding night there and fly to Lake Tahoe, Nevada, for a five-day honeymoon, with plenty of cash to spend. All paid for and arranged by Jacob's now-proud father, who was well aware that Janet's folks had barely been able to afford the wedding dress and gold wedding band for Jacob.

Jacob had psychologically prepared himself for the wedding night, the night of the consummation of their marriage, the night they'd always remember.

Up to now he had not been sexually attracted to Janet. Not one bit. Zippo.

But tonight should do it. If not now, never. It was do or die.

Jacob did the traditional carrying-the-bride-across-the-threshold thing while the porter held the door open. After he tipped the man, Janet dove into him. He too did the same. They kissed deep, wet sloppy kisses, kicked off their garments, rolled around nude like Adam and Eve on the king-size bed in the four-star suite.

Minutes of Janet's rollicking on him passed like hours. Her breathing was ferocious, her tongue swirled like a living entity over Jacob's body. She licked and sucked his toes, even. Then came the moment he had dreaded, even more daunting than having to engage in intercourse. Janet buried Jacob's semi-erect penis into her mouth, then proceeded to do a 180, placing her very moist, open sex directly at the area of his nose and mouth.

Jacob held his breath and shut his eyes. He couldn't be sure if he was even half erect any more. But he gave it a good oral go, licking inside and out. Janet's motions intensified. He breathed with his mouth and mouth only, fending off olfaction. His mind was a complete blank with the exception of the floating nude bodies of Mikey and Pat dancing above his head. He then moved on to the ripped non-beer-bellied dudes at his ex-place of employment, Olympian swimmers — the gods that they were — the statue of David chiseled by Michelangelo di Lodovico Buonarroti Simoni. Glistening, strong erections. Flat, hairy chests. The mysterious region under the scrotum. A celebrity-like smile with all white teeth on a beautiful young dude he'd once seen, an exquisite theophany of Adonis. He pushed, pushed, pushed all of them down and out, down into the garbage dump of thought-junk, out into the yawning dark pit of oblivion and the netherworld.

As Janet writhed with joy, Jacob fought, wrestling his muscular angels, struggling to cast them out.

They wouldn't go. They insisted on staying, as if they were saying to him, rather calmly, *Hey, we are your true nature. Why are you fighting us?*

No, they weren't his true nature, they were sodomite phantasms. Embodiments of lies, wickedness, perversion, *evil*. The church was right, they deserved to die, cease and be no more. Why, why must he have to put up with them? No wonder the church hates fags. He'd go on an anti-sodomite campaign at church one of these days after he'd become a preacher. It was his duty to bring the truth to the people. He wouldn't wish this on his worst enemy, this heinous struggle. May all men be free of it and rejoice in *normality*.

Janet came up for air, flipped around, kissed and licked his mouth where her sex had just been. How could she stand it? Was her ecstasy *that* elevated? It was inconceivable.

But there was no time for conceptualization. He was erect. Maybe it was because of the simple physical sensations brought on by Janet's motions. Maybe it was because he hadn't had an orgasm literally for weeks now since the time at the studio with Janet. Maybe it was because of the conjurations of *men*.

She got on her back, ready for him. Gasping, he lifted his torso from the bed with his arms, swung his legs around Janet's hips, and slipped his erection into Janet. He slid inside, deep, deep inside, all the way inside, with efficient ease.

Janet moaned loudly, eyes closing and opening, rolling them upward into her mind, absorbed, taken up to celestial spheres, to heaven.

He had to thrust, keep the sensation going. He didn't want to get flaccid. Not now, not during this momentous moment of consummation. It was his duty as *man* for his wife on this undefiled bed of marriage. The ecstasy was to be shared, the wondrous bliss of melting, blending into each other. Becoming One.

"*Pat*," Jacob whispered.

Janet's eyes opened wide in bewildered puzzlement.

"*Pah, hah,*" Jacob masked his involuntary exclamation of a bygone appellation.

Janet closed her eyes again, smiling her big, sweet smile, panting, huffing, moaning, writhing, covered in sweat.

Jacob too was sweating from the physical effort, but also from panic. He had to come, and fast, fast before the god Priapus decided to take a cigarette break due to the sheer psychic force and herculean mental and physical effort that was required to keep Jacob erect.

He had to be pragmatic. There simply was no choice. He thought of having sex with Pat, of being inside his ex-lover. That did the trick. Yes, he was making love to Pat. Thrusting into Pat. Deep into Pat.

Janet's hips lifted Jacob up. She opened her mouth wide and let out a high pitched shout. Jacob felt her inner walls pulsate. Pat was coming. Yes, Pat was coming, and yes, this was working, he too was coming.

His orgasm followed Janet's, about a minute out of synch. He released himself into her, picturing in his mind a refractive vision of boys and men he'd (un-)biblically known and seen.

Janet opened her eyes, half-lidded, a look of sheer delight on her shining countenance. She sighed a sigh of magnificent coital satisfaction, and laughed.

"What's so funny," Jacob asked rhetorically, out of breath, in somewhat of a whisper. He rolled over onto his back.

"Nothing," Janet said. "Nothing at all. Wow."

She turned to kiss him, he turned away.

"Nothing's funny is right," he said. Mind confused. Emotions chaotic, incongruous, wires crossed just about everywhere they could cross.

Janet hugged him. He slid out from under her, trudged to the shower, turned it on, walked in.

"Forgive me Jesus. Forgive me god. For I have sinned. I couldn't do it without thinking of men," he prayed in a whisper as the tepid water sprayed him. "Why, lord. Why? Why are you doing this to me? When will I ever be normal?"

He fell to his knees, started crying like a lost infant. Indeed, he was lost. The *normal* hadn't found him. Tonight was supposed to have been the night. He had been abandoned.

Janet opened the fogged shower door.

"What's wrong?" She said. "What's wrong, honey?"

"*Leave me alone!*" Jacob hollered, rising to his feet.

An uncontrollable psychotic rage welled up from unfathomable depths. He put his hands on Janet's neck, started to choke her. Choke the life out of her. Kill this thing, this hindrance, this living reminder that he couldn't, just *couldn't*, get excited over *woman*, that he still hadn't grown out of abnormality, out of wickedness, out of abominable evil.

His mind screamed: *I AM NOT A HOMOSEX-UAL!! I AM NOT WICKED!! I DON'T DESERVE DEATH!!*

But the moment he saw the look of terrified shock on her sweet face, the face that had basked in fulfill-ment just moments ago, his sensibility returned.

He released his hands. Janet gasped and coughed, rubbing her throat.

"What have I done," Jacob said. "Oh no, what have I done to you, Janet?"

Janet caught her breath, stared into Jacob's eyes.

"You choked me. You looked like you were crazy," she said.

"I was. I did go crazy. Janet. Janet, Janet, oh Janet. I did go crazy. Crazy. You make me crazy."

At that, the trusting soul Janet was, she smiled a slightly uncertain smile.

"I love you. I love you so dearly. I've never loved anybody like I love you. I've never made love to anyone before you. I had no idea, Janet, no idea. I had no idea it was going to be so intense. I must've been so psyched up. I don't even remember walking in the shower. The next minute I'm hurting you. I don't know what came over me."

"That's okay," Janet reassured him. "I was *so* ex-cited too. I guess men are just differ'nt."

"Yeah. they're different all right."

He pointed at his penis. Janet laughed. She didn't suspect a thing. Thank god.

This was bad. Very, very bad. It must never happen again.

He'd have to try to do better next time. Hopefully not too many more times before he'd become normal, enjoy it. This was his first time with a girl, after all. He just needed more practice. Practice makes perfect, yes, he'd come around to it.

So to speak.

8
Preacher Boy

The whole Lake Tahoe honeymoon was a nerve wracking affair for Jacob although his wife seemed to have let the momentary strangling insanity slide, as if it had never happened. For this, he was deeply grateful. But Janet's sex drive was fierce, she wanted to devour him every chance she could. This was a problem. He wasn't ready yet for all night sex-a-thons, considering the fact that he had to drum up male imagery in his head in order to stay hard and eventually ejaculate. On their first night together his sense of failure had driven him momentarily bonkers, out of his flippin' gourd with rage.

Where the hell had that rage come from? He wasn't one for blind, violent rage. The only times his kettle had boiled over were against his father, and only after lots of drunken abuse. Abuse he'd taken on the chin, feeling helpless, despised, his self-esteem going down the crapper which each passing insult.

The bathroom incident wasn't anything like that. In fact, it happened after what should've been a wonderful conclusion to a magnificent day. Nothing, absolutely nothing, had happened to provoke that kind of infernal furor. He had to reflect on it.

Number one, he'd never made love to someone of the opposite sex. He'd been nervous as all get go. But wasn't as if they'd never kissed, petted, and all that other premarital stuff good Christian couples do right before they get attached at the hips forever. But he'd never heard of normal guys losin' it, trying to choke their partners after sex. They'd smoke a cigarette and go for round two, or maybe even three if they had the stamina. After all that's how it was with him and Pat. He didn't want to choke Pat, did he? Of course not. So where did the outburst of anger come from, and why? If he were normal, and darned straight — so to speak — he was, wouldn't he have been blissful, like Janet was?

Number two, he, in pursuit of normal, had to fight off the demons of the male images of his past, and they proved a terrible hindrance on his wedding night. He wasn't angry at Janet, no, not at all, of course not. He was furious about those images, those memories, because they'd remind him that he was failing. He was failing nature, which in turn meant he was failing god. He was failing himself. He was failing Janet. He was failing his marriage.

Did he love Janet? Yes, he did. Of this he was certain. She was easy to love. She was going to be a good wife. A preacher needs a good wife. Not as a prop, no. But as his partner in god, that they may be

Christian exemplars unto the church, as models of how to live the moral, upstanding, biblical life.

Jacob dreaded their second night together, in that fine resort at Lake Tahoe, paid for by his father. He repressed thinking of boys and men and statuesque gods and male athletes, glistening workin' men without shirts. He psyched himself up, a kind of forceful self-hypnosis, telling himself that the flesh he desired was *woman*, particularly Janet, his wife, who was under him, above, all around him like an acrobat, practically insatiable, till he'd make her orgasm, as she'd lie down with her head on the pillow in deep contentment, eyes half-lidded, smiling.

The third night was much of the same. And though she wanted to make love in the morning, he jumped in the shower right quick, as they'd say back home, and got dressed to go to the lake for breakfast at the coffee shop. But she wanted him to enter her the third night. He let her harden him orally, then jumped on when he felt solid and close enough to the finish line.

The fourth morning Janet repeated the routine and he was able to make love to her like a normal man, meaning without having to conjure the unwanted images. They made love that night as well.

The fifth morning they got ready for their flight back to the city an hour outside of Dry Wells, where one of the church members'd promised to pick 'em up. Honeymoon days had been spent by Janet swimming and boating, she even went water skiing. Jacob stayed in the shade as much as he could, to keep from tanning, watching her from the shore.

She hadn't suspected anything. It seemed she'd completely forgotten about the horror in the bathroom.

Jacob was convinced now that normalcy had finally been bestowed upon him. No more wicked conjurations. He'd found a few tricks and methods that worked, it was all a matter of timing. After all he was healthy, and Janet's mouth, tongue, and hands would come to his aid.

He'd also come up with the brilliant idea that lovemaking should be relegated to once a week, on Monday nights. Four times a month he'd do his husband's duty, and that should be enough.

Janet didn't like the idea at first.

"*Once a week?* Why?"

"I'm going to be a preacher, Janet. A man of god. And although the marriage bed is undefiled, I also have to practice self control and a certain amount of chastity. I think once a week, on Monday nights, will be *our* time."

Janet stared off to space, in another direction.

"I s'ppose ..." she sighed.

The church granted Jacob a scholarship fund during his training, for they were grooming a new leader, a sidekick for Pastor Jim. It was enough to sustain him and Janet at the studio apartment for the duration of his studies, even without any extra income. They sure needed it since Jacob had quit his job at the country club. He was glad to have dumped the job, as he'd outgrown the inane banter, weed, beer, and

Tony, with whom he'd hardly exchanged a word since the rat-hole incident.

Jacob's father was being generous now too. He was the proud as a peacock father of a preacher-to-be, something he'd taken to bragging about at the country club. He even started showing up to church on Sunday mornings; he'd sold his share of the restaurant business to his partner, wrote Jacob a hefty check as a wedding gift to keep his son the preacher-to-be and pretty daughter-in-law afloat till Jacob started making money in the ministry. Once qualified, Jacob could substitute-preach for Pastor Jim when he was indisposed for whatever reason, on Sunday mornings and evenings. He would also be the opening speaker for Pastor Jim every Sunday morning with a short five or ten minute inspirational sermon; he would also do church administrative and financial work, and oversee the youth ministry in general. For this he'd be getting a monthly stipend.

To Jacob's surprise he was the only one who'd applied for the ministry training. There'd been a few trainee's in the past, but most members were happy with their day jobs — thanks to Reaganomic recovery — if they weren't on welfare or old 'nuff to be living off social security.

Staying out of the sun did the trick. Jacob walked in the shade whenever he'd have to step outside, wore a cowboy hat like many of the denizens in town to keep his face from turnin' tanned. He wore long sleeves in spite of the heat, and kept his hands in his pockets when the sun was overhead. Eventually he blended in with everybody else at church. Even Jedrik seemed okay with him now, which was a pleasant turn of events.

Jacob gradually developed the confidence and wherewithal to preach thanks to his disciplined routine; the once-a-week Monday night marital duty, daily studies, and three-times-a-week ministry sessions with elder Jesse.

Janet's period was late the second month into their married life, and the period never came.

Finally after three months of intensive studyin' and memorizin', learnin' about public speaking, the morning of Jacob's examination arrived. It was to be a private evaluation, doors closed to church members save Pastor Jim, six elders, and six deacons. They sat in the front pews, on both sides of the aisle.

Jacob couldn't sleep at all the night before, not a wink. He didn't want to let on that he was utterly exhausted, so he mustered up the last reserve of energy he had for his test sermon. He'd have to demonstrate everything he'd learned with respect to public speaking; he must quote scriptures, site them chapter and verse too, without looking at the bible. The requirement was that he show the total spectrum of what he'd learned in a matter of fifteen minutes. It was gonna be the longest fifteen minutes of his life hitherto, even longer than his wedding night, maybe.

Elder Jesse had a stopwatch; the panel was intimidating. They were all in suits, which showed respect for the process, the ministry, and Jacob. He too wore a suit, groomed himself impeccably with the help of Janet. They all had notepads in hand, which Jacob pretended not to see. He'd have to throw himself into the test. His future was riding on it, and the future of his family. Janet was two months pregnant but they hadn't told anybody yet. Now that he was up on the pulpit in front of the row of seasoned, exacting judges, he kinda wished they had. Maybe woulda softened 'em up a bit.

Time to bite the bullet, there was no wrigglin' out of it, no time for woulda, coulda, shoulda's.

The frightening panel just sat there, not sayin' a word. Not a smile, not a grin. Nuthin'. It was gonna be Jacob's show, all up to him, and he was gonna have to deliver.

Jacob cleared his throat at the podium. He looked at 'em, rememberin' the eye-contact thing.

"Good mornin' everybody. Thank you all for bein' here and for this opportunity. My lesson today is about the wickedness of sodomy."

He himself had chosen the subject for his sermon. Had deep feelings wrapped up in it, and had struggled with the whole concept himself, ever since the conversion therapy seminar.

Elder Jesse clicked the timer.

The panel listened with respectful, thoughtful attention, occasionally taking notes, as Jacob retold the story of Sodom and Gomorrah with dramatic embellishment and flare. The disobedience of the *woman* — yet again — who'd spun around to gawk at the destruction and had gotten herself turned into a shaft of sodium; he theologized somewhat in connecting that spectacular story to Mosaic law, that god didn't necessarily have to rain tarnation upon a land for homosexuality since its death penalty had gotten coded into the pentateuchal judicial system, which by Paul and other epistle writers had been reinterpreted in terms of same-sex on same-sex acts being punishable, though the method had not been specified. Either way the act was condemned severely in the old and new testaments. And Jacob also added Jesus's statement that *whosoever looketh on a woman to lust after her hath committed adultery with her already in his heart*, and thereby applied the same principle to sodomy, rewording it as: whosoever looketh on a man to lust after him hath already committed sodomy with him already in his heart. Thus one should expunge the heart of its wicked proclivities.

Elder Jesse clicked the watch and lifted his hand.

"All right, Jacob, thank you. Give us some time to deliberate. Wait out in the hall, we'll letcha know when we're done."

On that note, exuding confidence, Jacob thanked the judges and strode out of the auditorium, keeping mindful of his posture. He plunked down on the sofa in the hall, legs wobbly. His pits under his coat were drenched. Jacob closed his eyes and did some deep breathing.

Pastor Jim and the twelve judges were out within ten minutes, but it felt a heckuva lot longer.

Pastor Jim shook his head at Jacob, with a slight grimace. The others were lookin' somber.

Jacob's stomach fell to his ankles.

"Gotcha, didn't I?" Pastor Jim hollered, gave Jacob a light punch on the arm. "We ain't gonna scare ya any longer, Jacob. You did real fine. You've exceeded our expectations. Congratulations, son. You passed with fireworks."

Everybody laughed and congratulated him.

"The only critique we all had," elder Jesse added, "was usin' words like 'pentateuch' and 'judicial' — now I warned you 'bout those kinda words — but other'n'at, you had us riveted, I even forgot it was a test."

They all laughed and chuckled, shook Jacob's hand.

"I don't know what to say," Jacob said, and wiped a genuine tear. "Thank you all so much."

"Well yer one of us now," Pastor Jim encouraged him. "I got high hopes for ya."

"Thank you sir."

"I liked how you related the passage on lustin' in the heart to sodomy," one of the deacons said, "that was a home run for me."

"Thank you."

Pastor Jim informed Jacob that he'd be introduced next Sunday in his new capacity. He'd inform the congregation that Jacob was an administrator in training, that he'd passed the ministry course, would be opening every Sunday with a short lesson, overseeing the youth ministry in general, and sometimes would be preaching an entire sermon for the second Sunday evening service.

Jacob was officially a fledgling preacher boy, fired up 'n rarin' to go.

9
Lone Star

Their son was born in the spring of 1989. They had agreed that Janet would give him his first name and Jacob his middle, and that Jacob would have the honors of naming their second baby. To his chagrin Janet decided their son would be named Jubil, after her favorite granddad who'd passed away a few years back.

"It's short for jubilee," Janet glowed. "Ain't that a happy name?"

Jacob wasn't particularly fond of it. It wasn't a name he'd ever have conceived of naming his firstborn son let alone any son. He fought against the rather provincial soundin' name, argued that it sounded like *gerbil* and the kid'd get beaten up for it, but Janet wasn't budgin' n' 'at was 'at.

The church stipend was just enough for the couple, but with baby on board, expenses were higher. Jacob took a computer science and programming class at the community college outside of Dry Wells, surmising that the internet phenomenon would really catch on and so would the computer industry. If he could learn to navigate the computer world then he could, on the side, internally "wire" Dry Wells, particularly its establishments, increase business efficiency. That would be extra income for them, which they definitely needed now.

Their sex life was almost non-existent, had gone by the wayside, out the window. Even the once-a-week schedule was forgotten. The sexual heat had simmered down for Janet after Jubil was born, and Jacob was grateful that he had been relieved of the marital chore. It really had been a chore, a duty, something that he was required to do as a husband. His attraction to Janet had never come to pass as he'd hoped it would. Fortunately she didn't seem to give the matter too much thought, and had gone along with Jacob's sanctified explanation of why he wanted to "regulate" their sex life. She adored her son, couldn't get enough of him, devoted every waking minute to him and his needs. And for this, Jacob was grateful.

He opened with a short complimentary talk before Pastor Jim's sermon every Sunday, sometimes preached on his behalf in both Sunday services. The congregation was fond of him. Jacob's parents proudly attended Sunday mornings and evenings, his father, on the wagon even. Jacob oversaw some of the administrative affairs of the church and directed the youth group programs. He also taught bible classes on some Wednesdays, in the main auditorium, for the grownups.

Thus Jacob was busier'n a bee, with computer classes and church. The hectic schedule and workload was a blessing to him, even as estrangement toward his family gradually set in. Conflicting thoughts flooded his waking and sleeping consciousness on a constant basis now, with regard to why he could not get over his sexual attraction, no, attraction proper, to men. He was too busy now to lend any time or thought to his inner struggles. When things welled up, thoughts and fantasies about men, he pushed them down, down, down. Immersed himself further in scripture.

He cared, yes indeed he cared. Inasmuch as sex with Janet hadn't banished the demons, he railed and ranted against homosexuality in his sermons and bible lessons. His anti-homosexual emphasis was well appreciated by the heads of the church, touted as one of his outstanding themes of which he was fast becoming an outspoken expert.

Indeed, he cared. And he believed that somehow, by his outward, vocal condemnation of sodomites and sodomy, he was absolved of his sin, of having homosexual thoughts and desires over which he had absolutely no control. The only way god would forgive him was if he denounced it as often as he could.

And, it was not that his sex drive had waned, or had gone out the proverbial window with his sex life with Janet. No siree, all pistons were hammering full bore, sex drive was shootin' through the roof. Whence cometh relief?

He'd invested, discreetly of course, in several gay porno mags, literally kept them tucked in his closet, hidden in his luggage.

The more demanding his schedule became, the more slipshod his domestic life.

The weeks rolled by. It was several months before he got his certificate for computer programming. When he finally did, he sold his services to various establishments and businesses around and out of town, setting them up with computers, teaching them how they were used, creating custom programs for cutting-edge efficiency.

By the time Jubil was two and a half years old, Jacob was providing quite well for the family unit of three. Things were becoming financially solid. He qualified for a bank loan and purchased a home in west Dry Wells for them when Jubil turned three.

But there was the ever present inner conflict, which, sadly, was reaching a frenzied crescendo. He kept his self loathing in check even while he eyed some of the more attractive men at the businesses he'd frequent. There was no chance in hell he would jeopardize his standing as a minister of the church, especially as he was the community's leading proponent of everything anti-homosexual. The magazines and his right hand were his only outlet. He was bursting at the seams.

Janet was flesh and blood. Her sex drive had returned full force by the time Jubil was three. She tried to engage Jacob, tried to get him horny, to no avail. At all. In quiet desperation, as the saying goes, she lived from day to day, dreaming of sex, just sex in general, fantasizing now about other men, gradually, unconsciously, forgetting about Jacob.

Their marriage had become a sexless, unhappy sham, their communication had always been superficial and spotty at best. Nonetheless, they presented themselves to the church and business folks alike as one happy all-'merican Christian fam'ly.

The year was early 1995. Jubil was five, intelligent beyond his years, even spoke a little Spanish, a lil' bookworm, sharper'n a desert sticker, a chip off his dad's ol' block.

After one of her masturbatory sessions, solo-pleasuring herself with a cucumber while Jacob was at work, Janet became overwrought with guilt; she'd been fantasizing about several of the men at church taking her all at once. She'd reached her breaking point. Jacob was a goner, unavailable for counsel, comfort, or marital bliss. She *had* to talk to somebody, somebody wiser and more experienced than Jacob. *Cathlics* had the luxury of confessin' their sins to a priest, so she'd heard 'n known. Confession's good for the soul, so she'd heard.

Thus with Jacob perpetually at work, she approached Pastor Jim at his office one afternoon, while her mom watched Jubil. Janet begged Pastor Jim to swear to secrecy; asked him to keep everything she was about to say in confidence.

Pastor Jim gave her 'is word.

"I don't swear, Janit, but my word's good as gold. I'm here for ya."

Hesitantly and with great reluctance, she began divulging her marital problems to him. Then, the floodgates opened wide. She held nothin' back, went into explicit detail. The couple had had almost no sex since the birth of Jubil. She'd resorted to pleasurin' herself with objects around the house, vegetables even. She'd fantasize 'bout havin' two and three-somes with some of the men — she didn't mention who they were — at church. She'd been panicked when she croaked out that tidbit about fantasizing about other men. Fearin' hell and brimstone, spoutin' scripture with tears and snot runnin' down her face; *whosoever looketh on a man to lust after him hath committed adultery with him already in her heart.* She was sputterin' cryin, confessed to pretendin' a cuke was a hard erection, suckin' it and all. Wailin' asking if masturbatin' while married was a sin and on and on it went for nearly fifteen minutes.

Pastor Jim listened all the while Janet's eyes weren't even on 'im, just goin' on an' on 'bout stuff he'd ne'er expected ta hear from her, from any woman at church. His face was flushed red like a stoplight, blood rushed to every surface and extrem-ity, head to toe, particularly between his legs. He'd gotten stiffer'n a oakwood mace, seed risin' to the surface, spottin' his boxers, seepin' to the crotch of his trousers, makin' a spot the size of a quarter.

"I cain't take it no more, Pastor Jim. I'm goin' crazy. I'm a wife, see. I need lovin' like any woman, any wife would frum'er husband. But he ain't inter's-ted. Maybe he's impotent. What if he's impotent?"

She pronounced it syllable for syllable: *in-pough-tint.*

Janet wailed, cried. She'd lost all good-wife com-posure, just fell on apart, right there and then, in the presence of Pastor Jim.

"Now now, Janit. Come own now, don't cry."

He reached across the desk and pet her hair. He didn't wanna get up 'cause he knew the spot was gettin' bigger, knew she'd see his healthy, non-in-poughtint wood right pokin' from his crotch.

She cried without lettin' up, lettin' him pet her hair, feelin' touch. *Touch*, she'd been hungry, starvin' for touch. Just a touch. She couldn't even get that, not fer all the years since Jubil'd been born. She was young, had a strong sex drive. She'd wished she didn't but she did, and that's what husbands were for, but Jacob wasn't there. He wasn't there in their bedroom any more. He'd been long gone, absent.

She touched Pastor Jim's hand. Held it. Put his fingers in her mouth.

"Janit. Oh, Janit."

She dove out of her dress, unstrapped her bra. Pastor Jim jumped from his seat, started strippin' right quick.

Like a voracious lioness she dove to his crotch and sucked his wet, stiff erection as he groaned like he'd never done before, his sex life with his wife of twenty some years borin' as all git-go, he too pent up'n out of his ever lovin' gourd. Janet slammed her back onto his desk, papers n' books n' pens scatterin' to the four directions, wrapped her legs 'round his hips.

He lifted his body'n member up to her, inserted, kissed, lost himself in young, pretty, hotter'n fire pokers in hell Janet. They humped, thrusted, moaned, groaned, panted, squealed, sweated.

Then *pow*, he emptied his issue into Janet, into Jacob's wife, guilt comin' on now like gangbusters but too dang late. An ecstatic orgasm, Janet almost

screaming, she too experiencin' the moment of climax, simultaneous, together, in embrace, doin' the
forbidden deed, engagin' in adultery, breakin' god
and man's law, shatterin' 'em to pieces like Moses.

They huffed and huffed for a while, not breaking
their sinful embrace. Janet turned away and started
cryin' again.

"Oh lord. Oh lord, what have we done," Pastor
Jim lamented. "Oh dear lord, what have we done."

But the deed done been done an' 'at was 'at. They
both had everything to lose. This time he swore secrecy at the expense of hellfire. So did Janet.

Janet fell into a deep, inconsolable depression for
days after that. Her sadness wouldn't let up though
she tried keepin' a straight face to Jacob, and of
course was the same attentive mom that she'd always
been to her son. Divorce was out of the question she
knew, but she needed some time for herself. She decided to pack her bags and go to her parents' for a
while to think things over, explain the situation to
them. They'd be sympathetic, they'd understand.

After a particularly long day with clients, Jacob
came home to Janet in the living room watching TV;
Jubil was sawin' matchsticks in his room. She didn't
say a word to him. He tried to kiss her, as he always
did, but she didn't return it. When he entered their
bedroom to go use the shower, he saw that the magazines he'd tucked away in the luggage were laid out
on the bed. Dozens of 'em.

Nausea washed over him like a tidal wave. His
stomach and the whole world turned upside down.

He gathered them into a stack and headed back to the living room, dead man walkin'. He'd better think fast.

"Janet," he yelled. "What are you doing with this *filth?*"

Janet turned to him.

"What am *I* doin' with it?"

"That's right. Don't'cha know what these are?"

"Don't raise yer voice, you're gonna wake Jubil. Before I go, I'd like an explanation please."

"These are examples of the kind of pervasive evil and debauchery there is in the world. You don't think these are mine, do you?!"

He checked every nuance of her facial expressions, body language. She wanted to believe him. She very much wanted to.

"They belong to a member of our church. *Our church, can you believe that.* I swore to this person that I'd keep the whole disgusting mess confidential, because they very much want to turn a new leaf. They came to me for counsel, brought the magazines and asked me to destroy them. I was going to burn 'em, just hadn't had the chance to yet."

Janet's expression softened. It was working.

"I condemn sodomy and sodomites, Janet. You know that. You've always known that. *Of course* these repugnant rags aren't mine."

Janet nodded, stood up, and embraced him. He dropped the magazines. She kissed him; he kissed her back, deeply, passionately, full force. He stripped off her clothes, carried her to the bedroom as he had done on their wedding night, and mustered all his reserve to perform as a real, normal husband should on her. He shot the works, held nothin' back. Had to give it his all. His life depended on it.

10
The End

Languor, torpor, so the hours and days passed, as Janet's period stopped, as Jacob immersed himself in preachin' and workin', as Pastor Jim fervently preached nearly every Sunday on the subject of adultery and Christ's forgiveness. Husband-wife communication deteriorated to virtual nothingness, two people living alone together, flashin' their pearlies at church and social events as if they were the ideal 'merican Christian upstanding couple, the preacher, his wife and son, a picture of livin' the dream. Sex had come to a screechin' halt since the night Jacob's mags had been discovered.

And languish on they did, just dreamin', not really livin', just sleepwalking from day to day. Janet started suffering from debilitating depression. She'd contemplated hittin' the bottle like her folks once done, but thought better of it since she was with child and had a son who very much needed his mother. In large part because his daddy was absent in body and soul, only occasionally uttering the words they'd need to hear, every now and then when the timing was right.

A second son was born to the couple in the hot, again drought ridden summer of '96. As promised — not that Janet cared any more about it, about their marriage, about any of it save the future of her boys — Jacob chose his second son's first name. He opted for Justin, to stand for what is just and true, righteous in the lord.

Jacob's thrill at Justin's birth — which seemed genuine to Janet at first, though she ultimately came to believe it was merely because the second son anchored their family unit more, further entrenching her, — was short lived. She didn't care at all, as she felt it all slowly crumblin' to dust anyway. The boy was born prematurely, but as the months went by, he started to show whitish-blond hair on his noggin. Jubil resembled his father and mother both in genetic balance, but Jacob saw none of himself in Justin.

Jacob had dark brown hair, Janet's was chestnut. Both Jacob's parents had brown hair. There was no blond in his recent ancestral background. Janet's folks weren't blond either. From whence the blond?

Janet knew from whence the blond. One comforting aspect to Jacob's chronic familial absenteeism was that he'd have no inclination to delve into the mystery of Justin's blondness. His lookin' a little like his mom but nothin' like his dad would barely register on Jacob's radar. Though it was a comfort, a relief, it was also a source of anger and overwhelming melancholy for Janet. The whole thing.

Jubil was a mighty fine older brother to the little 'un, a built-in babysitter he was. He read books to him, watched TV with him, even spoon fed him babyfood after the breast-feedin' phase was over.

Their dad was crazy busy. He'd extended his services to the Soaptree Country Club, brokerage firms, banks, and other clients; word of mouth, his reputation for being the best man in town for the job, began to spread. He didn't come cheap but was worth it. He still preached, led bible studies, did finances and admin work for the church, directed the youth program.

It was a strategic busy-ness. He didn't want to be home, felt like a stranger there, especially to his second son. He didn't want to get dragged into sex with Janet. She'd be asleep when he got home late, which suited him right fine. Janet rarely cracked a smile anymore, but he was far removed from reflecting on such things. It was none of his business.

The young youth minister, twenty or so, who taught Jubil's age group on Wednesdays, caught Jacob's eye. Time to time they'd give each other knowin' looks, knowin' *what* of course was kept unsaid. But a mutual understanding was developing between them; subtle body language when they'd pass by each other, less subtle when they'd have one-on-one meetings about the syllabus et alia of the youth ministry.

Though his hectic schedule kept his sex drive at bay, it never went away. No sir, not a bit. He couldn't resort to magazines anymore, though he'd browse gay porn on the internet now and then, workin' his right arm. The virtual sex was drivin' him slowly crazy. Janet was goin' slowly crazy.

Yes sir, Jacob wanted the youth minister. But what was he to do? The boy knew Jacob was a sodomite-basher *par excellence*. And yet the boy would give him those looks, whenever he could. Those looks of interest. Carnal interest. Sexual attraction.

Thus, the time had come, winter of '97, indeed it had to, when the dam finally broke. One Saturday after a meetin' with the young man. The church buildings were empty. They'd both found themselves in the men's room. Just sorta gravitated there.

They exploded onto each other. Stripped their clothes, wrasslin', kissin', lickin'. Jacob turned him around, bent him over the sink, spat on his erection and inserted.

But alas, alas, though he'd finally had his pecker in the lad's ass, in walked Pastor Jim.

The action stopped, freeze frame, frozen for eternity, right there'n then. Stopped cold, cold as the Arctic glaciers.

Pastor Jim's mouth hung open. The preacher just stood there. Speechless. Aghast. Shocked. Mind-boggled. Steam comin' off 'im like a coal-driven locomotive. Volcanic eruption.

"WHAT IN THE NAME OF HELL ARE YOU DOING?"

* * * * *

It was over.

Jacob was excommunicated, as was the young man.

Jacob couldn't face his wife with the news. He'd come home and had embraced Jubil and wept. Wept bitterly. Jubil also cried, cried his eyes out, not knowing why.

"Take good care of your mother and brother, Jubil. Don't forget that I love you, always. Daddy has to leave for a while. But you'll see me again someday soon."

"Where are you goin' dad? Why you hafta leave?"

"I've got business to do out of town. I'm just gonna miss you, that's all. Don't cry, I won't be gone long."

Fortunately Janet was sleeping when he said his farewell to Jubil. She'd been sleeping a lot. Jacob didn't go into the bedroom, Justin was probably in there sleeping with her.

He didn't bother packing. Wallet and car keys, computer tower from his office. He dashed out of the house.

"Bye dad," Jubil hugged his father's leg. "You'll be back soon, right?"

"I will," Jacob was about to lose it again. "I will. Take care of mom and your brother. I love you."

He checked the rearview mirror and saw Jubil standin' there wavin' on the driveway in front of their home. His ex-home. His facade.

He vanished from dry ol' Dry Wells, never to be seen or heard from again.

11
Apocalypse

He'd resigned himself to havin' lost his soul, fallen from the grace of god. He'd been a hypocrite, a sodomite, a fake, a charlatan, a failure as a husband and father, and a liar. The inner voice of god was gone. He'd been abandoned, just like he'd abandoned his family, left them in the lurch. Janet could sell the house, pay back the bank the remaining mortgage, live off the remainder. She could also live for a couple years off the balance in their joint bank account. He'd only withdrawn enough to get himself a small, inexpensive apartment in Seattle, the basic necessities needed to start his life over with a clean slate.

He tried his darnedest to keep the scenarios that were likely unfolding back in Dry Wells from invading his thoughts. O the scandal it must've been. Janet's heart, shattered. His parents and Mitch devastated and humiliated, father fallin' off the wagon for good, his in-laws in an uproar, the church wantin' to lynch 'im, and Pastor Jim kickin' up a shitstorm of fury.

Fuck Dry Wells. Fuck Pastor Jim. Fuck the church. They were all a bunch of desert rats.

He'd contacted the clients that weren't affiliated with church members in any way, letting them know he had to leave town for good for personal reasons; made recommendations to them of other able people in the field, and the clients were good with that. They'd also written recommendations for him that he'd requested, as fast as he could before word of the scandal got out. Secular folks probably wouldn't care as much, but they were still all Christians without a doubt. Dry Wells was practically all Christian and most would be spittin' mad about havin' had a sodomite in their midst.

Within a week after settling into his apartment — he'd rushed like a runaway train — he landed a job as a programmer in Bellevue, half-hour commute from his new residence. A stroke of good fortune it was. He was set.

Having been abandoned by god, having abandoned pretty much all that he'd built and destroyed hitherto, he set to reinventing himself. His life in general, his identity. He had his middle and first names swapped and legally changed along with his last, still went by Jacob to his peers and coworkers claiming it was actually his middle name; and indeed it now was. After all, Jubil was smart and might eventually start trying to track down his father. The breadcrumbs had to be swept away.

Changed names, changed location, changed job, changed life, dead faith: what remained intact? Two things. He was attracted to men. And, he firmly believed he wasn't gay.

After all, homosexuality didn't exist in nature as a natural biological propensity; when homosexual behavior would happen, and happen it would, every instance of it was aberrant. Science and the bible were in agreement about that. Those conversion therapists from the seminar he'd attended lifetimes ago had approached the problem from secular psychological perspectives and had reached the conclusion that homosexuality was a scientifically diagnosed psychological disorder of sorts. It was a matter of choice to indulge the sickness or overcome it. *Ergo*, there was no such thing as a naturally born homosexual; there was only the aberrant homosexual proclivity, the choice, the either-or to act on the disorder or take refuge in natural, normal, god-created heterosexuality. Everybody by nature was heterosexual.

Syllogism:

Jacob is a man.
Man was created heterosexual by god.
Therefore, Jacob was created heterosexual by god.

Quod erat demonstrandum, Amen, axiomatic. Theorem, lemma, conclusive scientific facts and biblical truth rolled into one Aristotlean package of simple logic. So at the end of the day he was just a stunted boy. The homosexual inclinations and proclivities were nothing but his inherent laziness and cowardice, indicative of his fear of growing up. It was all very scientific, really. And consistent with the bible's teachings.

But what the heck. Since he'd absconded from the past, nobody would be policing or keeping tabs on him now. Although the time would come when his natural heterosexuality would dawn on him as he ripened with age, maturity, and wisdom, he could — and perhaps *should* — get it out of his system.

It didn't take long for Jacob to start frequenting gay bars, having one night stands. Booze and drugs helped numb his guilt. Guilt that he, a straight man, who knew his homosexual preference was simple psychological laziness and cowardice, and maybe even just a deeply rooted fear of *woman* — had his mother molested him when he was little? Couldn't be. She'd always been passive, had almost no initiative of her own — would continually indulge the others in the same boat as he, only harboring the delusion that they were gay when in fact they were straight by nature, by god's design. Guilt that he didn't try to convert them, lead them to the lord and savior Jesus Christ so that they might be saved, so that they might renounce their gay delusion and walk the straight and narrow as he someday would. Guilt that he was still a fake, a pretender, as he'd always been all throughout his Dry Wells stint, insofar as he had always been masquerading, only now as a gay man.

The gay community: they were all deluded ghosts who didn't exist but believed they did. Jacob too was a ghost, but he at least had the edge, that he knew he was choosing to be one. Homosexuality was a choice, this much he knew. For now he just couldn't resist it, was making up for lost time, had to have his catharsis, purge it from his life once and for all. Method: go for it, because it was provisional therapy and nothing more. It was the only way for him now, to exorcise the gay ghost.

By 2001 *anno domini* his therapy method of one night stands and medication (mostly booze, weed, XTC) had taken him far down the rabbit hole, all out debauchery on weekends and sometimes in the middle of the work week. He'd gone to work countless times, in a lingering substance stupor. The therapy hadn't been working. His unnatural homosexual tendencies hadn't dissipated. They'd only intensified. No heterosexual desire in sight, not even a little curiosity. And guilt, oh boy. Getting plastered on booze and drug cocktails would provide temporary relief in the form of utter oblivion, but the next day, forget it. How long had he been doing this now, five years? Five fucking years without result, getting more entrenched, more lost, more guilty. *My god, why hast thou forsaken me.*

Tuesday morning on September 11, 2001. Jacob was still feeling the effects of the night before, too much to drink. He'd been surveying the wares at one of his cruisin' haunts but had just window shopped; too tired, a little too tipsy, too numb. He'd downed a few more vodka-tonics before bed, woke up five hours later with a monstrous headache. Commuting to work felt like hell on wheels, so to speak, but he managed, thanks to a couple hits of pot and the rather odd fact that there were hardly any cars on the free-way.

The security guy, a fixture at his desk wasn't there; nobody in the lobby. Nobody in the elevator going up to his floor. Too weird, but he felt too sick to ponder the mystery. The headache was gone by the time he trudged to his cubicle, but the lethargy, guilt, and melancholy remained. The office was almost empty for some reason. What the hell was going on, was it a national holiday he hadn't heard about? As he pondered the wretched state of his misery a co-worker scrambled into the quiet office, looking as though the end of the world had come.

"Oh, Jacob. I thought I heard somebody come in. Shit, what are you doing here?"

Jacob looked up at the guy.

"What? What do you mean what am I doing here?"

"Haven't you seen the news? We're at war." His voice warbled; the guy was trying to keep from crying, unsuccessfully.

"*What?*"

"We're in the employee lounge, come on."

Jacob was too sick to talk or work, was contemplating taking the day off, he was just sitting at his cubicle in a delirium anyway, but he couldn't question the urgency in his coworker's voice. He got up fast, room reeling and ceiling warping, and joined the small group watching the tube in the lounge.

Smoke was rising out of one of the Twin Towers in New York. The anchor was explaining that what appeared to be a large passenger plane had crashed into the skyscraper, a terrible accident of unprecedented horror. One of Jacob's co-workers gagged and ran to the bathroom when the footage on the TV showed somebody jumping from the burning building. Then almost immediately after, another large plane swooped into the south tower and exploded. Shouts and screams could be heard in the background; the plane had smashed right through Jacob, his psyche, his soul. And soon the buildings crumbled from the top down with nightmarish speed in infernal clouds of smoke. The scene switched to the devastation at the Pentagon, then to news about a hijacked plane that went down in western Pennsylvania.

Confusion, chaos, miasma, horror, anger, sadness: the office, no, all of America, bore witness to the end of the world as they had known it.

Sheer dread took over.

Jacob stumbled out of the office building, staggered like a fucked up drunk to the bushes, and vomited. He hyperventilated, got in his car, drove home. The freeway was almost empty still, now he knew why.

He poured all his booze down the kitchen sink, tossed his bag of weed and container of ecstasy in the toilet, flushed it. *Twin.* The twins had collapsed into dust. He had been *twinned*, separated at birth, a split between who he really was and who he'd chosen to be. Judgement had come, the wrath of his god had made its advent.

Jacob slammed his knees to the floor, bowled himself over, clasping hands, forehead to the floor. He was trembling. He was sickened, sick. Sick in mind, body, and soul.

Please, he wailed, tears gushing. *One more chance. Just one more chance, dear god. Dear Lord, my savior.*

Two days later, precariousness pervading the air, Jacob watched and trembled as Pat Robertson interviewed Jerry Falwell, a reverend of inscrutable high moral rectitude. He'd been watching nothing but the news and Christian TV since that terrifying Tuesday morning. Even the reverend, a righteous man, said he'd humbled himself before god, as had all the church members and students of Liberty University, in a gathering of prayer. Jacob fell to his knees as he listened, shaking. Praying in silence, praying in incoherent mutterings. America had a new enemy: "Islamic fundamentalists, radical terrorists, Middle Eastern monsters," as the man of god put it.

The two leaders of men, prophets of god in these end times, were hoping the horror of September 11 would catalyze an American spiritual renewal.

"What we saw on Tuesday," the reverend Falwell said, "as terrible as it is, could be minuscule if, in fact, God continues to lift the curtain and allow the enemies of America to give us probably what we deserve.

"The ACLU has got to take a lot of blame for this — And I know I'll hear from them for this — successfully with the help of the federal court system, throwing God out of the public square, out of the schools, the abortionists have got to bear some burden for this because God will not be mocked and when we destroy forty million little innocent babies, we make God mad. I really believe that the pagans and the abortionists and the feminists and the gays and the lesbians who are actively trying to make that an alternative lifestyle, the ACLU, People for the American Way, all of them who try to secularize America: I point the finger in their face and say you helped this happen."

Jacob ran to the toilet to vomit. Utter dread, fear such as he'd never thought possible. The TV volume was loud enough. He had to listen, keep listening to god as he spoke through men, the kind of men he had once aspired to become.

"I totally concur," Pat Robertson said, "and the problem is we've adopted that agenda at the highest levels of our government, and so we're responsible as a free society for what the top people do, and the top people, of course, is the court system."

"Pat, did you notice yesterday that the ACLU and all the Christ-haters, the People for the American Way, NOW, etc., were totally disregarded by the Democrats and the Republicans in both houses of Congress, as they went out on the steps and called out to god in prayer and sang *God Bless America* and said, let the ACLU be hanged. In other words, when the nation is on its knees, the only normal and natural and spiritual thing to do is what we ought to be doing all the time, calling on god."

Yes. Yes, reverend. I call on thee, my god. Do not forsake me. I repent. I repent of my sins, of my sodomies, my debaucheries, my wretchedness, my carnal want of men's flesh. Please, god, please, Jesus, I am not at fault for what happened that Tuesday. Had I known that would've happened, I would have

*never left Dry Wells, I would have tried harder, with
all my heart and soul, to be normal as you — thou —
hast created me, all of mankind, to be.*

Prayed hard he did, on his knees, flopping down,
rolling around to the left and right like a Pentecostal
holy roller, wailing, *smiting his breast*, gnashing his
teeth. If he'd had a potato sack he would've torn it
and tied it around his bare chest as a token sackcloth.
Repentance was everything now, forgiveness and
mercy. *My god, speak to me. Show me a sign of thine
forgiveness.*

And harken, a still small voice.

Well well, the voice of the almighty creator spoke
forth. *Thou prodigal, thou at last wishest to return
unto our fold, to partake of eternal life in heaven.*

Ah, he's back. The tears fell from Jacob's eyes
like Seattle rain.

*It is good to hear you in my heart again, my god.
It has been so long. Father, my father, I want to come
home.*

The inner voice of the god he had known so well
as a child replied:

*We so loved the world, that we gave our only be-
gotten Son, that whosoever believeth in him should
not perish, but have everlasting life.*

Overwhelming spiritual comfort washed over Jacob. He sat back up on his knees, bowed his head
with chin to chest, eyes tightly shut.

If thou desireth everlasting life, the inner god
said, *cast off thine inner strife. Believest thou that
thou art gay?*

*No, my dear god, I am not gay. I know there is no
such thing.*

Thou art darn tootin' correct, hence why hast thou kicked against the pricks?

My spirit is willing but the flesh is weak, dear father. I have indulged my childishness, I have behaved foolishly and unnaturally. I repent.

That there's the sorta drivel thou hast spewed the last time we had spoken. We awaited thine arrival at the pearly gates, thou never showed up. Are we to believe what thou sayest now?

Please believe me. I was frightened, I didn't want to drown. I couldn't go through with it. Please forgive me.

Well, the inner god said, *we shall forgive thee for old time's sake, then. But we have one condition.*

Here he goes again with the one condition — Jacob thought — then immediately dispersed the intrusive mental retort.

We heard that. We know thine thought spam, beware. We knowest all thine thoughts.

I'm sorry! I'm sorry, Jacob wailed and smote his breast.

Anyhoo, back to the one condition. Thou must go back to Dry Wells and attend Sunday worship at thine church where thou wert busted for having lusted, and henceforth got the boot from the coot. It won't be a hoot, but well, shoot, that there's the one condition. Easy 'nuff, ain't it?

Go back to Dry Wells and attend Sunday worship at my old church? But why, god?

Thou needest the closure so thou canst regain composure. Obey this unburdensome command and we shall let bygones be bygones. We shall let thee slide.

It was a daunting command. But perhaps getting closure would do him good. After all he'd hightailed it outta there in a mad flurry, had never turned back. Yes, the time had now come to turn back, and hopefully, he wouldn't be turned into salt.

I will do as thou sayest, dear god. I promise to follow through this time.

And of course we assume thou won't resume butt piracy ever again.

Never, dear god, never. I will get therapy.

Fine, then. Have a nice trip. Hasta luego!

Jacob had racked up enough paid vacation. He bought an overnight round-trip ticket to the city north of Dry Wells. Incognito he'd go, but he'd go, because he'd promised god he would. Back to his church to attend service for whatever reason god had in mind, to have his sins absolved in return so that he may, lord willing, start anew, afresh, slate wiped clean by the blood of the lamb.

Since he hadn't shaved since nine-eleven, he figured he'd better keep the scraggly look. Hadn't had a haircut in over a month either. Perfect. He'd put on a pair of shades and sit in the back of the church auditorium. It'd been long enough, people wouldn't have him on their minds; nobody'd recognize him. And if they did, well, he'd just dash out like a bat out of hell.

The purpose of the trip was the promise he had made to god, a token of his repentance which would lead to his renewal. He would go back to the place where he'd had a modicum of contentment, where he'd earned communal respect from the church, the business world, and even the desert rats. The place where he preached from the pulpit and had his family. It was a token trip, nothing more was demanded by god but that he attend Sunday worship at his old church in Dry Wells. And needless to say, that he never engage in homosexuality — in thought or practice — ever again. The command of his god made more and more sense the more he thought about it. By going back to the spiritual roots of his maturation into adulthood, he could reclaim that which had been left undone. Was it possible that he could reclaim more than the strictly spiritual? Could he go back to how things were, back to his wife and children, even? Since he'd left the dustbowl five years ago, his family had ceased to exist as far as he was concerned. They were a dream of a dream, a previous life to which he had died. Died, dead, gone, buried. But could it be resurrected? Could it be, by some amazing miraculous chance, he might be able to reclaim his former life? Is that why god wanted him to return to his spiritual provenance?

Jubil was the only one he hadn't been able to will into the oblivion of the forgotten. That boy was exceptional. So kind, so intelligent, so full of *joie de vivre*, hungry to learn, practically bilingual. Jacob was grateful that Jubil had the church and youth ministry, so that he might learn the ways of the word, seeing as how America, the Christian nation was now at war against Islam. The future was precarious and uncertain and he'd need the church and god's word to be his guide. Indeed, Jubil had guides far better than his lost father in his life now. Maybe someday Jubil would even join the lord's army and fight the lord's holy war, for America's freedom. Indeed, the same for his younger brother, the strange boy — he'd be five now — Justin would also have the church and the lord's word as his guide. May his sons become fighters for freedom and the lord.

Like the impact of an unforgettable image resurfacing from a forgotten dream, the scenery, just flat expanses of sand, snapped him back to when he'd first stepped foot on the Martian landscape of Dry Wells. He was an extraterrestrial back then, and was now, all over again. His alienation was to be revisited by divine design. Jacob told himself that driving by his home in west Dry Wells and his parents' home in Soaptree would be necessary if his quest for closure and self reflection were to be complete. And maybe, just maybe, a miracle might somehow come to pass.

Even the higher-end of west Dry Wells looked worn, cracked by harsh solar rays. Shitty economic downturns had taken a considerable toll on the area. Potholes still plagued the main highway's pavement, only worse for the wear.

Jacob could feel his blood pressure rise as he approached the once familiar terrain of his ex-family's neighborhood. All was intact as if nothing had changed. He drove at a crawling 5 MPH by the house he had abandoned, an eternity ago. Two cars and an SUV were parked in the driveway; an elderly gent was washing one of the cars with a bucket and sponge. Jacob braked and rolled down the car window.

"Excuse me sir, do you live here?"

The man stopped what he was doing and stared at Jacob, expressionless.

"Whut?"

"I'm sorry, do you live here?"

The man turned toward the house, as if to check if he was in the right place.

"Sure do," he said. "What can I do ya for?"

"I'm looking for an old friend who used to live here."

"Oh," he said. "What's 'is name?"

"She. Her name's Janet."

"Janet? She don't live *here*."

"If I may ask, sir, do you know a woman by that name?"

"Nope," he said, "sure don't."

"I see. She used to live in that house with her two children, I was just wondering."

"We been here almost four years now," he said. "You got the wrong house."

It wasn't the wrong house, but it was obvious now that Janet had sold it.

"I guess so, it's been a long time. Thank you just the same."

The man waved and went back to sponging.

Well, that was that, Jacob thought. It was one kind of closure, although a somewhat disappointing one. No miracle here.

Next, before finding a motel, he wanted to make the thirty-minute haul to Soaptree Country Club. Everything seemed smaller along the way, miniature compared to how he'd experienced it all those years ago when he was still brimming with hope and ambition.

Ol' Soaptree Country Club was in shambles. The security gate was gone, the relatively opulent zone had degenerated into just another overexposed residential acreage of desert. The country clubhouse, that once elegant and exclusive pride of Knobs county, had been shut down. Arid wilderness had taken over the once green, well maintained golf course, now blended in with the *desert*. Many of the homes looked abandoned or foreclosed on. Soaptree Country Club was dead.

As he inched his rented sedan along the path by his parents' home, he was struck by the realization that they too had moved, were gone, or had died. A FOR SALE sign was posted out front, and there was no sign of life within. *The abomination of desolation*, Jacob thought to himself: Nebuchadnezzar's Babylon had fallen. Fallen on hard times, fallen from the paradisal heaven that was once its Reaganomic stronghold. All that remained after the ravages of time had torn through like a leisurely tornado was desolation, and his parents had been swept away. And Mitch, that plain and simple younger brother of his who would sometimes enter his memories like an extra in a movie, must have gone off to college on a sports scholarship or something. Who knew. They'd never been close, and Jacob hadn't missed him. He hadn't missed his parents either for that matter. He'd never missed Janet or Justin even, never missed the church or anyone in it. Jubil was another phenomenon altogether, but Jacob's severance from his first son was the necessary collateral damage for having to start his life all over. Yep, his life had been a series of fits and spurts all right.

No miracle here either.

Sunday morning he deliberately went a little late to the church service, parked the rented car in the church parking lot. It was filled with vehicles different from those in Seattle. He hadn't given it a thought while he lived here, he'd realized, but almost all the cars were gas hogs: vans, large pickups, SUVs, as if their owners were taking a stand in support of *big oil*.

The lobby was empty, thank goodness, everybody was already in the main auditorium. Mercifully, it was an usher he'd never seen before who greeted him and handed him a program. This was something new. No programs were ever handed out when he'd been part of the church. The congregation, on their feet, was reciting the Pledge of Allegiance. As everyone sat down in unison, Jacob took a seat furthest back, close to one of the exits. He glanced at the pamphlet, just a piece of paper folded in half. The title of the morning's sermon was: *America at War*.

And lo, there he was on stage in his signature white three-piece suit, shiny shoes and red tie: Pastor Jim pacin' the stage, both hands holding *the word* behind him, lookin' deeply worried, serious, and concerned.

I'm here, lord, just as I'd promised. I am here to do my penance, take communion, and leave with my sins forgiven. I want to be righteous, lord, to fight the good fight

Curtailing his inner prayer, Pastor Jim's voice boomed into the recesses of Jacob's soul, reverber-

ated like a *deja vu*, flooding him with an instantane-
ous montage of encapsulated memories.

"America is at war!"

The audience was hushed as if at a funeral service.

"Brethren. Our brethren of the faith, wives, children. Yes, America, the one nation under god, *our*
nation, is at war. Our Christian nation, founded on the
bible and the faith of the fathers of our Constitution,
is at war."

He paced nervously on stage, starin' at the floor.
Suddenly he looked up.

"Did we declare it? Did we ask for it?"

Several people in the audience shouted *No!*

"Well, lemme ask ya this *agin*, then. *Did* we ask
for it?"

Nobody said a word this time.

"I'm gonna tell ya somethin' hard to hear. This
ain't easy for me, folks. But we *did* ask for it. How
did 'at happen?"

Dramatic pause.

"I'm gonna tell ya how. Another dramatic pause.
By *tolerance*. Now you've all heard that word said
many, many times. In the lib'ral media, why, even in
schools, and even *here* at the lord's church."

Pervasive silence.

"I ne'er, and I mean *never*, have I ever used that
word. Because I knew, folks. I knew. I knew that in
the lord's good time, and yes, the time did come on
nine-eleven, that he'd make his displeasure known to
us all. We'd gotten complacent, see. We'd grown *tolerant* as a church, as a society. As a nation. I myself
as a servant of god, of our lord 'n savior Jesus Christ,

have fought hard *aginst* it, but didn't fight hard 'nuff. You been deceived, brethren. *You* have believed the lib'ral lies of the 'merican Civil Liberties Union: the hogwash of *tolerance*.

"Well, I'm done, folks. I'm done toleratin' toler-ance. It's war. *Ame-ri-cuh*, the greatest nation in the world and e'er been in the history've the world, is under attack. Who's attackin' us? *Islam* terrorists. But what happened on Tuesday mornin', that there was jes god's wakeup call, see. He's shown us his *dis-playzure*. What's god so displeased 'bout? *Tolerance*.

"Why did god destroy Sodom and Gomorrah? Did god tolerate 'em?"

A goodly number of members shouted *NO!*

"*Hell* no. Oh, pardon *me*, folks, pardon me. You ain't ne'er heard me swear. But I'm *mad*, see. And *god* is mad, and yew, all of you, need to get *mad*."

Pause, overall silence.

"No sir. The time for bein' nice is over. The time of toleratin' is over. Why? Tell me *why*, then, if god doesn't tolerate, who're we to tolerate? Are we bet-ter'n god? That there's a dumb question, ain't it?"

He flipped open his bible.

"First Corinthians five, six to eight: 'Your glory-ing is not good. Know ye not that a little leaven leav-eneth the whole lump? Purge out therefore the old leaven, that ye may be a new lump, as ye are unleav-ened. For even Christ our passover is sacrificed for us: Therefore let us keep the feast, not with old leaven, neither with the leaven of malice and wicked-ness; but with the unleavened bread of sincerity and truth.'

"Folks, we *gloried*. We gloried, been gloryin', been sittin' on a skillet, toleratin', lettin' things *be*. Yer gloryin' ain't good. Ain't good, see, cuz a little leaven leavens the whole lump. Does apostle Paul say to tolerate a little leaven?"

NO! members yelled.

"'at's right. 'at's right brethren. No. What's he suggest we do? *Suggest?* He ain't suggestin'. He *commands* us: *Purge out the old leaven*! Purge. *Not* tolerate. *Purge*."

"Amen, praise god," "Amen, thank you Jesus," multiple praises by members went up.

"And *what* is the old leaven? Says so right here: the leaven of malice and wickedness. And what kinda of leaven is that? It ain't a *what*, it's a *who*. Homosexuals. Christ-hating' Lib'rals. Abortionists. Feminists. Lezbiens. Undesirables. Jews.

"No, the time of toleratin' is over. We gloried in our tolerance for a good while, too long a while, 'an look what happened. We didn't purge 'em, and we, 'merica, got leavened.

"We need to become a new lump of unleavened bread, brethren, wives, children. An' I'm sayin' this, that when I mean purge, I mean *purge*."

Amen! members shouted.

"We're at war. Do soldiers *tolerate* their enemies in war? *Hell no!* They see an enemy, an' —" he made the gesture of rat-a-tat-tattin' with an imaginary machine gun.

"*Purge*. Terrorists have declared war on 'merica, on *us*. Do *they* tolerate us? *Hell no!* They wanna see us destroyed. And *who* are these terrorists? *The Islam?* Yes, but they ain't all. No, no, no …"

Pastor Jim's voice trailed off. Pensive pause.

"No folks, there's more. Lots more. You all been *toleratin'* so long you forgot. Let the leaven spoil the whole lump. Why, Jesus din't tolerate 'em greedy Jews at the Temple in Jerusalem, did he? No. He whipped 'um, turned their tables over, 'n kicked 'em out."

"Praise the lord." Praises resounded throughout. Jacob also whispered *thank you Jesus*.

Pastor Jim whipped open his bible to another page.

"Matthew ten, thirty-four ta thirty-nine. 'Think not that I am come to send peace on earth: I came not to send peace, but a sword. For I am come to set a man at variance against his father, and the daughter against her mother, and the daughter in law against her mother in law. And a man's foes *shall be* they of his own household.'

"Mark eight, thirty-four ta thirty-nine: 'He that loveth father or mother more than me is not worthy of me: and he that loveth son or daughter more than me is not worthy of me. And he that taketh not his cross, and followeth after me, is not worthy of me. He that findeth his life shall lose it: and he that loseth his life for my sake shall find it.'

"I call these passages the lord's declaration of war. A war against every *enimee*, even father, mother, son, daughter if need be, if they ain't worthy of our lord and savior Jesus Christ.

"Now some'a yew, suma you might be thinkin', *why, Pastor Jim, din't Jesus say to turn the other cheek? Din't he say we should love our enimees?*"

This Pastor Jim said with an effeminate, mamby-pamby tone of mockery, his left wrist limp.

"*Sure* he does. But is there any contradiction in the word of god?"

NO! many yelled.

"Of *course* not. What's the lord mean then?"

Pause. Silence.

"I'm gonna tell ya what it means. The lord is sayin' we turn our cheeks to our *brethren*. For the house divided against itself cannot stand. Ain't that right? Ain't that right, folks? We don't fight among ourselves. *We* ain't the enemy. Our *enimees* are sodomites, lib'rals, abortionists, feminists, undesirables, Islam, the Jew, an' *all* unbelievers. Didn't the lord bring a sword, not peace? Ain't that what he said? Are we s'posed to *tolerate* 'em, turn our cheeks at 'em an' say, *go on, go on now, destroy our land, destroy our country, destroy the nation of god?* Of course not! *Take up yer sword 'an fight!*"

"Amen," "praise the lord," "thank you Jesus."

"If ya see a terrorist, anybody at all suspicious, why, do watch'a see fit as a citizen of god's nation. Take up yer sword. Call the authorities if ya have to. Keep vigilant, keep yer eyes peeled an' yer ears open. *Take up yer sword an' fight!*"

YES! Amen!

"*Love your enemies?* Well, that there's a lil tricky, see. But'cha gotta remember, there ain't no contraction in the word of god. So what could that mean? I'll tell what it means. It's about *tough love*. By destroyin' the flesh of yer *enimees*, yer doin' 'em a favor. First Corinthians, five-five: 'To deliver such a one unto Satan for the destruction of the flesh, that the spirit may be saved in the day of the Lord Jesus.'

"Now *that*, folks, is the love that surpasseth all understandin'. Have a look at Exodus thirty-two, twenty-six to twenty-seven: 'Then Moses stood in the gate of the camp, and said, Who is on the LORD's side? let him come unto me. And all the sons of Levi gathered themselves together unto him. And he said unto them, Thus saith the LORD God of Israel, Put every man his sword by his side, and go in and out from gate to gate throughout the camp, and slay every man his brother, and every man his companion, and every man his neighbour.' They *slew* three thousand of 'em."

Pastor Jim made a gesture of hackin' with a sword, bible in same hand. The auditorium was *a-hush*.

"Brethren. Wives, children. You all been tolerant too long. You been fed lib'ral lies, been fooled by their hooey."

He paced thoughtfully, back an' forth.

"There was a time. There once was a time, a long, long time ago, when men didn't tolerate. You all hearda Martin Luther, haven't ya? Not *that* Martin Luther, I'm talkin' 'bout the *real* Martin Luther, a fighter who fought for the word of god, for our lord and savior Jesus Christ, against the antichrist Catholic church. I'm gonna read ya what the courageous warrior of god wrote."

He took out a folded piece of paper from his bible, unfolded it, and read:

"*What then shall we Christians do with this damned, rejected race of Jews? First, their syna-*

gogues should be set on fire, and whatever does not burn up should be covered or spread over with dirt so that no one may ever be able to see a cinder or stone of it. And this ought to be done for the honor of God and of Christianity, in order that God may see that we are true Christians. Secondly, their homes should be likewise broken down and destroyed. Thirdly, they should be deprived of their prayerbooks and talmuds in which such idolatry, lies, cursing and blasphemy are taught. Fourthly, their rabbis must be forbidden under threat of death to teach anymore.'

"'Now whoever wishes to accept venomous serpents, desperate enemies of the lord, and to honor them, to let himself be robbed, pillaged, corrupted and cursed by them, need only turn to the Jews. If this is not enough for him, he can do more: crawl up into their — and worship the sanctuary, so as to glorify himself afterwards for having been merciful, for having fortified the Devil and his children, in order to blaspheme our beloved lord and the precious blood that has redeemed us. He will then be a perfect Christian, filled with works of mercy, for which Christ will reward him on the-day of judgment with the eternal fire of hell, where he will roast together with the Jews. If I find a Jew to baptize, I shall lead him to the Elbe bridge, hang a stone around his neck, and push him into the water, baptizing him with the name of Avraham. I cannot convert the Jews. Our lord Christ did not succeed in doing so; but I can close their mouths so that there will be nothing for them to do but to lie upon the ground. I hope I shall never be so stupid as to be circumcised; I would rather cut off the left breast of my Catherine and of all women. If we *are to remain unsullied by the blasphemy of the Jews and not wish to take part in it, we must be separated from them and they must be driven out of their country.'"*

The audience was quiet. Pastor Jim folded the sheet of paper, tucked it back in his bible.

"An' there's one more, from another famous Christian. I won't say who, but here it is."

He opened his bible, read from a card wedged in it:

"'*I believe that I am today acting according to the purposes of the Almighty Creator. In resisting the Jew, I am fighting the Lord's battle.'"*

Pastor Jim's bible flapped shut like a fly catcher snappin' up its prey.

"Psalms hundrid thirty-nine, nineteen ta twenty-two: 'Surely thou wilt slay the wicked, O God: depart from me therefore, ye bloody men. For they speak against thee wickedly, and thine enemies take thy name in vain. Do not I hate them, O LORD, that hate thee? and am not I grieved with those that rise up against thee? I hate them with perfect hatred: I count them mine enemies.' An' finally: Luke eleven, twenty-three: 'He that is not with me is against me: and he that gathereth not with me scattereth.'

"You're either for us or aginst us, an' if yer aginst us, yer our enemy. And like Martin Luther, the *Christian* Martin Luther, we can't tolerate wickedness no more, or else we'll be goin' down with the ship. The ship of *fools*, that is. Be outspoken, tell it like it is, an' act like ya mean it. Take up yer sword'n fight.

"If I weren't so old I'd go enlist in the army. *Sign me up*, right quick. All you young men, join the army, the marines, the navy. Dun't matter. Serve the nation to protect it, and thus you serve god an' Jesus, an' his church. This is a holy war, the Islam got *that* right. But our *enemeez*, the terrorists, are all who've brought *calamatay* upon us, the leaveners, the unclean, the enemies of god: sodomites, lib'rals, abortionists, feminists, *lezbiens*, undeseriables, the Islam, the Jew."

Pastor Jim looked down at his feet, then back up to the stage lights overhead that illumined his countenance.

"Now you all might be wonderin': *Why, Pastor Jim? Why did ya read us the speech by the great, real Martin Luther about Jews? Isn't America at war with the Islam and terrorists? Jews ain't terrorists.* You all might be wonderin' that. Well I'm gonna tell ya about this war, something all of yew need ta know. But first, let me ask ya this. Who owns the lib'ral media? Who owns the lib'ral Hollywood? Who calls the shots on the *left* coast?"

Many members nodded in understanding, shouting *Jews!*

"Jews. 'at's right. The Jew owns the lib'ral media, where all the evil propaganda comes from. They *tolerate* abominations of the *left coast*, don't they? Think 'bout it, an' think real hard, folks. Why, ya see, you already know. Don't take a whole lotta thinkin'. The Jew, the natural enemy of Christ, the murderers of Christ, the murderers that called fer the blood of our lord ta be upon 'em, *they* are responsible fer spreadin' lies about *toleratin'*. The government caved in, public schools caved in, the ACLU got cree-ated, an' the people of 'merica, swallered their lies whole hog. So what's 'at tell ya folks? what's 'at tell ya?

"I moan tell ya. 'at tells ya that if yer *tolerant*, yer followin' the doctrine of the Jew, and *NOT* the doctrine of god, of Jesus."

Amen!

"Our war," Pastor Jim paused, pondered. "Our war, brethren, wives, children. Our war is not only against flesh and blood, but against principalities. Ephesians six-twelve: 'For we wrestle not against flesh and blood, but against principalities, against powers, against the rulers of the darkness of this world, against spiritual wickedness in high places.'

"We wrestle against spiritual wickedness in high places. 'at there's where all the lies come from. From the enemies of Christ. 'an the biggest lie, is *tolerance*. Does god want us to *tolerate?*"

NO!

"Years ago we, *our* church, had sodomites in our midst. One of 'em, a young man barely twenty years old, committed suicide after his wickedness was exposed.

Jacob's stomach flipped over.

"He got caught red handed with another abominable sodomite, right when they were lustin' on each other like a coupla wild monkeys. If 'at were now, if 'at were today, when we're now at war against spiritual wickedness, why, I would've shot 'em myself."

Yes! Amen!

"The boy did right to kill 'imself. I don't know what happened t'other 'un, but if I ever saw 'im agin, why, he gone wish he'd ne'er met Pastor Jim."

Jacob trembled. Acid reflux, cold sweat. *He killed himself. It was my fault.*

"Leviticus twenty, thirteen: 'If a man also lie with mankind, as he lieth with a woman, both of them have committed an abomination: they shall surely be put to death; their blood shall be upon them.'

"What's 'at say, brethren? What's 'at say? Does god say, *'they shall surely be tolerated?'*"

No! Several men also yelled *Perverts! Child molesters! Kill 'em!*

Pastor Jim chuckled, let out an exasperated sigh. Jacob was frozen in fear.

"Ya know, people are sayin' AIDs, the homo disease, could be eradicated by the year 2020 and all that. Why, it can be eradicated by Christmas, at least a goodly amount of it. Just round up the homos and kill 'em."

The auditorium burst into laughter.

"Or just round 'em up in a large fenced area, drop 'em food by *helacopter*, and they'll soon die off 'cause they won't be procreatin'."

More laughter.

"The book'a Genesis says god created Adam n' Eve, not Adam n' Steve."

Laughter.

"Just thinkin'a kissin' 'nother man makes me wanna puke."

Uproarious laughter all around. Jacob wanted to puke.

"Genesis one, twenty-eight: 'And God blessed them, and God said unto them, Be fruitful, and multiply, and replenish the earth, and subdue it: and have dominion over the fish of the sea, and over the fowl of the air, and over every living thing that moveth upon the earth.'

"Be fruitful and multiply, replenish the earth, subdue it, dominate it. That there's our mission as god's creation, ain't it? We been *commanded* to subdue n' dominate the earth. What's that tell ya folks? Ya can't obey god's commandment if yer homo, now can ya? Ya can't subdue earth and dominate it if yer a bleedin' heart environmentalist lib'ral can ya?"

No! "Praise god." "Thank you Jesus."

"First Corinthians six, nine to ten:" Pastor Jim flipped his bible open: "'Know ye not that the unrighteous shall not inherit the kingdom of God? Be not deceived: neither fornicators, nor idolaters, nor adulterers, nor effeminate, nor abusers of themselves with mankind, Nor thieves, nor covetous, nor drunkards, nor revilers, nor extortioners, shall inherit the kingdom of God.'

"The effeminate, the abusers of themselves with mankind, they're the homos, the sodomites. Romans one, twenty-six ta twenty-seven: 'For this cause God gave them up unto vile affections: for even their women did change the natural use into that which is against nature: And likewise also the men, leaving the natural use of the woman, burned in their lust one toward another; men with men working that which is unseemly, and receiving in themselves that recompence of their error which was meet.'

"Romans one, thirty-two: 'Who knowing the judgment of God, that they which commit such things are worthy of death, not only do the same, but have pleasure in them that do them.'

"An' when I say those who are wicked are worthy'a death, I ain't making it up. *We,* brethren, even wives an' children, must rise and fight. It's a war. We're at war, 'merica's at war, and we must take up the sword an' fight. Jesus didn't bring peace, he brought a sword. We got fat 'n sassy bein' tolerant fer too long. Tolerance ain't the way to fight a war. Don't believe the falsehood, the wicked lies of the Jew, the media, the ACLU, the lib'rals. No more of 'at. 'merica believed 'em an' god sent the attacks on September eleven. Let us rise up an' fight the holy war, take up arms and show 'em why we're the greatest nation in the world, a Christian nation, a people pleasin' ta god. Let us pray."

All rose from their seats, bowed their heads, and prayed silently in tandem with Pastor Jim's closing prayer. Jacob prayed with everyone, with his church again. Pastor Jim's sermon was disturbing but poignant. Jacob could never, *ever,* go back to sodomy again. His days of wickedness were over.

Jacob gazed here and there as the ushers brought around the crackers and grape juice for the communion, he recognized nobody except a few elders, deacons, and their wives way up front near the stage. No Janet, no Jubil, no Justin. He probably wouldn't even recognize Justin if he saw him. Didn't matter, he knew he wasn't there to revive an old life long gone; he'd come back simply to stoke the fire for the new, and Pastor Jim sure had done it.

Soon as he sipped the grape juice and prayed along with the closing prayer Jacob scrammed out the back door into the parkin' lot. He was queasy, dizzy. Heart pumpin' like he'd just run a mile.

A young boy was standin' by his rented car. Jacob smiled and nodded to him. He wasn't the age Justin would be, and he would've recognized Jubil; the boy's age was somewhere between the age of his two boys. As Jacob pulled the keys from his pocket, the boy moved closer.

"Where ya goin', mister?"

"I'm goin' home. You shouldn't be out in the parking lot by yourself, go back inside."

"Inside where?"

Jacob clucked his tongue.

"The church. Go back in the church."

"I don't go ta church, mister."

Jacob looked the boy in the face. His eyes. They both had a different color: one grayish blue, the other, almost pure white. Jacob suddenly recalled the dog that had followed him for hours back to Soaptree the day he'd ditched school.

The boy's presence felt ominous. Jacob looked away, opened the car door. He started the engine and pulled out of the spot just as the others started walkin' to their vehicles. The boy kept staring at Jacob. He checked the rear view mirror as he turned out of the lot, indeed, the boy was still watching as he drove away.

12
The
Gay Science

I

Some things were crystal clear now. Jacob couldn't go back to Pastor Jim's church or his family. Ever. The past had been sealed once and for all. Perhaps that was why god had commanded him to make one final visit to Dry Wells. There was another clear purpose to the visit, which was implied in Pastor Jim's sermon. Jacob must eradicate all homosexual inclinations, walk the path of righteousness — this time for real — and enter the lord's ministry again. He'd have to move from that Sodom and Gomorrah Seattle, from the "left coast" as Pastor Jim had put it. America was at war, and a hotbed of god's displeasure was no place to be. He'd move to the vicinity of Dry Wells, maybe less than a hundred miles out of town somewhere where nobody'd heard of 'im. He would start over, from scratch.

Fortunately he'd saved up enough money to pack his bags and leave Seattle for good. He could take his job skills anywhere, that wouldn't be a problem. He could get outstanding references from his managers and clients. Jacob gave his job in Bellevue two weeks' notice. They were sorry to hear he had to go, but he couldn't wait to *git*; he requested that his remaining paid vacation serve as his final two weeks.

On his knees at his apartment he prayed, supplicated for guidance. He then took a pencil, closed his eyes, and jabbed a spot on the map within the state wherein lie Dry Wells. Lo and behold his pencil had landed on Pozo Secos, sixty-six miles north of Dry Wells. Population: much larger than Dry Wells. Good. To Pozo Secos he wouldst go.

He researched the town online. Job prospects would be a'plenty, at least for him. It wasn't too podunk, wasn't too metropolitan either. Just the right place to get started.

Jacob fell to his knees and prayed again. He got up, went to his computer and typed 'conversion therapy pozo secos'. The very top entry was Calvary Conversion Therapy Center. This was going to be it. He checked their website, seemed to be run by reputable people with PhDs. But most importantly, they were Christians, and the therapy was bible based. He didn't want that left-coast secular stuff he'd once had a sample of. He needed something solid. There were various options for the length and type of therapy, to be determined on a case by case basis. Sounded level headed, reasonable.

He called them right away; a man answered, kindly, gentle, understanding voice. Polite. Had a slight twang, which was charming. Jacob set up an appointment for his preliminary session, four days hence.

Amazingly, in the five years he'd lived as a "bachelor" he hadn't acquired much of anything with the exception of a nice dining set, desk, wares, some decent clothes and shoes. Home, his apartment, had basically been just a crash-pad. It made things easy for moving, though. He didn't care about the material things; nothing he couldn't purchase again. Money wasn't a concern, knock on wood. Just as when he had fled Dry Wells, he'd be leaving again with a very light load.

He mapped out his route and drove southward, rightward, away from the left coast, toward his destination and the new stronghold of hope: Pozo Secos. He'd have to do the same song and dance there, get an apartment, a job. It'd be far easier this time. He wasn't an escapee. Wouldn't have to change his name, fearful people might be looking for him, afraid he'd get no or bad references. Hadn't left behind a trail of ill repute, nobody in Seattle or Bellevue wanted him dead.

He drove fourteen hours a day, slept at convenient motels. Went to bed with a prayer, rose with a prayer. He'd been praying hard, mostly for the conversion therapy to work. It'd have to. He'd been a very, very eschatologically late bloomer, but blossom he would, yes sir, yeah, even unto normal heterosexuality. And once he'd cured himself of this condition, his illness, he'd enter the ministry again. Start his own church in a rented space somewhere, maybe even have good old fashioned tent meetings, get the ball rollin'.

On the day of his appointment Jacob was good and ready, having had a solid night's sleep at a nearby motel. He paid for three nights upfront, hoping he'd find an apartment in the interim. He didn't get much chance to see the city at night, but liked what he did see. Lots of churches, decent looking restaurants, business establishments. Things were looking O-K.

Calvary Conversion Therapy Center was a surprisingly clean, church-like contemporary structure, a fine looking place; his ticket to wellness. He was greeted at the desk by the same chap who made his appointment over the phone. Quite professional he was, politely thanking Jacob for coming, giving him a sheaf of forms to fill out, asking how his trip was, how long he was staying, and so on. He was pleasantly surprised to hear Jacob intended to stay for good, but asked no further questions.

There was a questionnaire that needed filling out after the personal identification and medical history forms.

Religious preference/ affiliation/ faith **Christian**

Why are you interested in conversion therapy? **I want to be well, become normal**

Have you ever have undergone conversion therapy? **No** *If yes, explain* _____.

How did you hear about us? **Internet search**

Have you ever felt out of control? **Yes**

Are you on medication? **No**. *If yes, list prescription(s)* ___.

From a scale of 1 to 10, 1 being not very and 10 being extremely, how strong are your sexual feelings toward people of the same sex? **10**

Have you ever had homosexual contact, relationships? **Yes** *If yes, explain* **Multiple partners, no serious relationships, started when I was 16**

Have you ever had sexual or intimate relationships with members of the opposite sex? **Yes** *If yes, explain* **With one woman, she was my wife (not officially divorced)**

Do you struggle with feelings of inferiority? **Yes**

Have you ever been sexually abused / molested? **No** *If yes, explain* _____.

Have you ever considered or attempted suicide? **Yes**

Do you have thoughts of wanting to harm yourself, or are you suicidal now? **No**

And so on.

It took him a half an hour to fill everything out. After signing the bottom of the last form and a waiver, Jacob handed the man behind the desk the papers, showing him his Washington driver's license.

"Thank you. Please be seated, the doctor will be out shortly."

"Thank you."

Minutes later an older gentlemanly sort, tall, dark hair, clean shaven, maybe in his fifties or early sixties, appeared in the lobby to greet Jacob. He wore a suit, could've passed for a preacher, politician, or metropolitan mogul. He put out his hand.

"Jacob, welcome to Calvary Conversion Therapy Center."

Jacob shook his hand, very firm grip. A *man*'s grip. He didn't release Jacob's hand.

The fellow behind the desk handed the doc the clipboard, which he took with his left hand, keeping his eyes on Jacob's all the while.

"I'm Doctor Keester Johnson, and it's nice to meet you."

Jacob hesitated a moment, wasn't sure if Keester was kidding. If he wasn't kidding his parents were sadists and he must've had a helluva rough childhood.

"How do you do, it's nice meeting you, doctor."

Doc finally let go the shake.

"Well, follow me to my office."

The space was reminiscent of a hospital minus the wards. They walked down a hall, turned right down another short hall; Dr. Johnson's office was at the far end of it.

The office room was well decorated, arranged, and furnished with a psychotherapy-like sofa. Banal prints of generic-looking sceneries were ensconced on the walls, along with smatterings of degrees, certificates, and awards. Daylight flooded the room through the large window behind his desk. One tall wooden bookcase neatly displayed all kinds of psych books: 'Homosexuality' was in the title of many of them. Jacob's overall impression of the clinic, Dr. Johnson, and his office space gave him a quick Gestalt that all was legit, reputable.

He seated himself behind his desk and smiled as Jacob sat across from him in the only other chair.

"So, tell me a little about yourself, Jacob. I have your file in front of me but I want to hear it from you in your own words."

"Yes," Jacob smiled, "where should I start?"

"From the beginning. We have all the time in the world, Jacob. This is the free initial consultation, you're not on a clock."

With that green light Jacob recollected and relayed everything that might be salient to his case, holding nothing back, making no pretenses. He had to stop a few times along the way to cry it out. Dr. Johnson was patient and kind. Dr. Johnson scooted a box of tissues across the desk to him.

"Jacob. Listen to me carefully. Are you listening to me?"

He looked up at the doc, nodded, blew his nose like a kazoo.

"You are only partially responsible. You made choices because of your illness. Your illness is what compelled you. Your male partners were suffering from the same disorder. It's a case of sick people behaving symptomatically."

Jacob nodded, though he took no comfort in his words.

"Sadly, I've known a few men who, overcome by social pressures, opted to end it all. They didn't have the option you had, of escaping to start over somewhere else, in relative anonymity as a man without a past. But instead of starting over to become well, you chose to indulge your sickness, your disorder. Now when I say 'disorder,' that is exactly what homosexuality is."

"Yes, I know," Jacob sniffed. "It's a terrible sickness, and I *hate* it."

"Homosexuality is a disease. The *Diagnostic and Statistical Manual of Mental Disorders* published by the American Psychiatric Association in 1952 listed homosexuality as a mental disorder. Some of the greatest minds in psychiatry, Sigmund Freud and Carl Jung, viewed homosexuality as a mental disorder. Unfortunately, due to liberal political pressures the entry was removed from the manual in 1973. You could argue that that was the beginning of the rampant, unbridled spread of the disease. God, in his wrath, smote with AIDS, and again, with the terrorist attacks on September eleven, a day we must not soon forget.

"There are secular organizations such as the National Association for Research and Therapy of Homosexuality — they go by NARTH — who work with Christian organizations and clinics such as ours, but without the element of faith, Christian faith, I don't believe a cure can ever be complete."

"I agree," Jacob said, tossing the wadded tissue into the trash.

"Nice shot," Dr. Johnson smiled. "Until the early 80's, lobotomies and chemical castration were used as a means of curing the disorder. The techniques are no longer legal, and in my opinion rightfully so. They are far too intrusive and completely unnecessary. Why? Because I myself didn't need a lobotomy or castration, but was cured, nonetheless. With Christ all things are possible, isn't that so?"

"Yes, doctor."

"And I'm living proof, that with faith and dedication to wellness, we can be cured of this terrible disease that is so displeasing to god. I assure you, Jacob, that when you competed your treatment, you will see the world with new eyes. You will be free. Disease free, acceptable to god, acceptable to the world."

"Nobody wants to be sick unless they enjoy the attention they get for being sick. When I see a gay pride parade on the news, I see unwell people parading their sickness, embracing their disease, not even knowing they are truly ill."

"Yes."

"You are a Christian as am I. Evangelical, like you, brought up in the church. I am a recovered, ex-homosexual. And when I say 'homosexual,' I am speaking of a psychological disorder. After having tried to hide my desires for many years, I too was caught in the act. That was when I decided enough was enough, and I took to undertaking conversion therapy. That was almost thirty years ago, Jacob. And I have never gone back to being sick again. I have three grown children, and a wife of thirty years."

Jacob smiled. A ray of hope.

"Yes. It works, Jacob. Conversion therapy works. I wanted others to recover as I did, so I got my doctorate in psychology with that goal in mind, to some-day open my own practice, my own clinic, affiliated with the best conversion therapy institutions the world over. I've implemented the techniques that cured me, and all of the therapists here are thoroughly trained and adept at applying them. The results have been remarkable. Certainly there have been patients who have reverted, but most of them return for what we call a booster."

"That's very reassuring, I can't wait to get started."

"Now, down to brass tacks, the practical side of things. Based on my diagnosis and the answers in your questionnaire, my recommendation is inpatient treatment. Our two-week treatment, which is the most comprehensive. In my decades long experience in the field, I've seen the best results from the inpatient program. I myself completed a two week treatment at the center that cured me. Outpatient programs can be effective, but more boosters have been necessary in those cases. I understand if you have work and cannot take two weeks off, but I strongly recommend that you make a commitment, if not now, very soon, for the two-week inpatient program."

"Oh that won't be a problem," Jacob grinned. "I read about it on the web site. I've come all the way here with the intention of doing the full program."

"Good. Very good, Jacob. I'm very glad to hear that. As for fees and —"

"The payment," Jacob smiled.

"Yes. Unfortunately since homosexuality is no longer considered a mental disorder, our treatment is not covered by medical insurance. Everything will be out of pocket. But if you have some financial hardship, there are organizations and churches that will supplement the fees, up to a good portion of the payment."

"How much is it?"

"Fifteen-thousand. Dollars, not *Pesos*," he smiled. "I know it isn't inexpensive, but our track record being what it is, I would say it's worth every penny."

Wow, Jacob thought. But that was okay.

"I can afford it. I'll cut you the check right now. Fortunately I have a healthy savings account, courtesy of the bachelor workaholic."

Dr. Johnson laughed.

II

Jacob checked out of the motel the very evening he had checked in, no refund for the extra two nights he'd paid for up front. He loaded his luggage back into the car and took off to Calvary Conversion Therapy Center. A different man checked him in this time, but he too was cordial, welcoming.

To his delight, his room for the next two weeks, on the second floor, was better than the motel. Well, he figured, for fifteen-thousand bones it better be decent. But he dismissed the monetary cynicism as fast as he'd thought it. He was here for treatment, to get well, get disease-free.

He slept soundly that night; slept better than he'd slept in who knew how long. Before dawn he'd snapped awake on his own, showered, prayed, and went to the lounge downstairs to wait for breakfast.

Breakfast was served at 7:15 a.m. Lunch was at 1 p.m., dinner at 6:00 p.m. He'd checked the daily program, a slip of printed paper among his welcome-package materials. The schedule was the same for all fourteen days with the exception of Sundays, worship taking the place of Session 1:

06:30 Rise
07:15 Breakfast (light)
08:00-10:00 Session 1 (except Sunday: chapel worship service)
10:00-11:00 Break
11:00-13:00 Session 2
13:00-14:00 Lunch & Break
14:00-16:00 Session 3
16:00-17:00 Break
17:00-18:00 Session 4
18:00-19:00 Dinner
19:00-21:00 Group counseling
21:00-22:00 Session 5
22:00-23:00 Bible study (personal time for prayer and reflection)
23:00 Lights out

Two other men joined him for breakfast in the lounge room; food was brought on trays by staff members wearing plastic gloves. The men, Jacob discovered in cordial conversation, were outpatients on their respective programs. Jacob was the only inpatient, somewhat of a rarity, he was told.

He wasn't surprised. It was an expensive program after all, and severe cases like his must be rather scarce. He learned there were three other men on the outpatient program who'd be joining them for the evening group session.

"Today's day twelve," Troy, one of the two outpatients said as he sipped coffee. "I'm tellin' ya, Jacob, it's Jacob right? I already feel like a new man."

"That's so fantastic. I can't wait to get started, today's my first day."

"I know," he chuckled, "it's gonna be tough, but stick to it. I started feeling the difference after five days. Just five days!"

"Is Doctor Johnson your therapist?"

"No, Doctor Cross. The clinic has a dozen qualified therapists. They prefer to administer treatments one-on-one but I've heard they'll double up if necessary."

"Does it ever get that crowded?" Jacob asked.

"I don't know. Probably not."

The patients went to their respective therapists and treatment rooms on the first floor at 8:00 a.m sharp. Doctor Johnson was wearing a suit, with a white smock over it this time. The room was rather small, no windows, made Jacob a tad claustrophobic. Only thing in the room other than a lit counter with a sink in it, was a table with two fairly comfortable chairs on either side. The table was partitioned by a large computer monitor turned toward the seat Jacob took; keyboard and mouse were on the doctor's side. Other miscellany on the Doc's side; unopened bottled water, a small orange prescription container, some unidentifiable gizmos with wires coming out of them, and a brown leather bound King James Version holy bible. Oh, and a cylindrical plastic bin with its lid opened, lined with a plastic bag, stood right next to Jacob's seat.

"Welcome to your first session, Jacob. Welcome to the first day of the rest of your life." Doctor Johnson grinned his toothy bright-white grin. "Are you ready?"

"I'm ready. Ready as I've ever been."

"Good! Let's start with a prayer."

They held hands across the table, bowed heads.

"Heavenly father, we thank you for today, for another day we may live in peace and freedom in your great nation, even as our young soldiers fight to protect us away from their homes; we pray for them, O lord, we also pray for our police force, who watch over us, who protect and serve us day and night, and for all civil servants who work toward making the world a more peaceful place, pleasurable to thee. They are our heroes, O lord, and we thank thee for our heroes who fight for our lord and savior Jesus Christ, his word, his blood of atonement for our salvation. Today we also give thanks for our clinic founded in your name, in your word, to cure the world of the sickness of homosexuality, to bring souls unto Christ, to bring bodies and minds to purity, to wellness, mental and physical health, even unto the hope of marriage with the opposite sex, to do thine will and replenish the earth. We thank you, lord, for Jacob, that he has the resolve and initiative to have come to your blessed clinic, to become freed of his life of mental illness. We pray for the success of his treatment, for complete and total healing, and for the forgiveness of his sins, and our sins. In Jesus's name, amen."

"*Amen,*" Jacob punctuated in unison, with gusto and determination.

Dr. Johnson was preparing this and that on his side behind the monitor, Jacob had no idea what to expect first.

"Now, before we begin, I want to explain the process of our treatment. Based on behavioral science, it's a reward and punishment process of reinforcement. As the process goes on, your body learns first that its reactions to certain stimuli, which it found pleasurable before — and which it finds pleasurable *now* — are incorrect reactions. And stimuli which the body had previously found and currently finds *no* pleasure in, will in turn become pleasurable. In other words, your responses to certain stimuli will become reversed. You could say it's an osmosis process of teaching your body to react in such a way that eventually your mind will follow suit. Do you have any questions?"

"No, I am aware that the treatment entails behavior modification."

"Good. Before we start, and this will be daily, once with each session, I want you to take this medication here with the bottle of water," he handed Jacob the water and a small pill from the container. Jacob swallowed it down.

Dr. Johnson reached over to the lit counter, opened the cabinet and brought out a plastic object that reminded Jacob of a dog or cat feeder, one bowl for water and the other for kibbles, except much deeper; this one, however, had water in both bowls. One side had plenty of ice, the other side no ice. Dr.

Johnson laid a large, thick towel in front of Jacob, set the object on top.

"First, I want you to dip your hands into the side with the ice water, and keep your hands in there. Tell me when it becomes uncomfortable."

Jacob complied. The water was extremely cold. After a few minutes, Jacob vocalized his discomfort.

As if on cue, on the monitor flashed two studly lookin' shirtless dudes with cop-staches wearing low-rise jeans, bodies sweaty and chiseled like Roman statues. Jacob's heart skipped a beat. They were gorgeous.

"Hey, Chaz."

"Hey, Tad."

Chaz and Tad high-fived each other, and talked about putting up drywall. It was the typical 90's cheese-fest, an appalling caricature of gay behavior. They were construction workers working indoors on what appeared to be a house in progress. Chaz bent over to pick up some tools, and Tad slid his hand into the back of Chaz's pants.

"Stop," Chaz said with a highly pronounced 's'. "You savage."

Who makes this shit? Jacob wondered. But the two men weren't hard on the eyes.

And thus began the groping, kissing, licking, sliding out of their jeans, displaying solid, well-oiled erections which they rubbed on each other as if they were rattling sabers.

Although he was sufficiently aroused by the scene, Jacob was distracted by the stinging pain in his hands. By the time Tad mounted Chaz, Jacob could endure the pain no longer. He closed his eyes.

"Don't close your eyes!" Dr. Johnson exclaimed. "Watch the screen. You must never take your eyes off the screen."

Jacob opened his eyes and continued watching the hump-fest.

"How are your hands?"

"I don't think I can take it much longer. I feel like I'm getting frostbite."

"Okay, now put your hands in the bowl on the right."

Jacob quickly complied. Immediate relief; the water was rather warm, comforting.

Immediately the scene changed to a man and woman Jacob's age, man in tuxedo, woman in wedding dress, in the bedroom. Brought back honeymoon memories. They smiled at each other and kissed. Deeply, passionately. The scene cross-faded into the couple fully nude on the bed, man caressing his wife's breasts tenderly, then the man fell out of the scene; only the woman's body could be seen. The camera panned from her breasts to her stomach, the slender curves of her waist, her pubic region, her thighs, her feet; the camera was following the man's hand as it brushed her tenderly.

The scene was banal, boring and meaningless. Jacob was still thinking of Chaz and Tad, hoping maybe to see another shot of the nude husband.

"Put your hands back in the left bowl."

Jacob dipped his hands back in the ice water; there hadn't been sufficient time for them to warm up. Dr. Johnson took an ice bucket out of a small fridge embedded in the counter, scooped more ice over Jacob's frozen hands.

Chaz and Tad came back on screen, continuing what they had been doing before the scene had changed to the honeymoon suite.

The same process was repeated, only this time, Dr. Johnson directed his movements without asking if his hands were feeling uncomfortable or in pain. Having no say with regard to when he could dip his hands in the right bowl added to the stress and anticipation he was feeling.

With every repetition the duration in the left ice-bowl seemed to get longer while the man-woman sex-scene relief got shorter. After the fifth repetition Jacob let out a slight burp. It felt like acid reflux; then came nausea.

"Left bowl," Doctor Johnson said.

Jacob dipped his hands in the left bowl.   He fought back vomit while Chaz sucked Tad's stiff cock, ramming it down his throat with zest, saliva running down from his chin.

The pain in his hands was becoming excruciating, the nausea overwhelming.

"Excuse me doctor I —" Jacob threw his breakfast up into the cylinder.

Dr. Johnson scooted a box of tissues to him; Jacob wiped his mouth.

"Hands back in the left bowl."

The so-called "process" was ninety minutes, the last hour being that of nothing but Chaz and Tad, pain, nausea, vomiting, and dry heaving.

Dr. Johnson handed him a small paper cup of white liquid. Soon after he downed the potion, in just a matter of minutes, the nausea was gone.

"Right bowl."

From Chaz and Tad the scene changed to the hubby and wife kissing, making passionate standard-sex-position love on the bed. The woman moaned in delight and ecstasy.

Thank goodness, the nausea was completely gone; in fact he felt a little euphoric. Hands felt warm and comfortable in the tepid bowl of water on the right side.

After watching the couple make love for approximately ten minutes, with the angles of the shots strategically designed to focus on the woman's nude body, face, mouth, hair, the scene whited out into a scene of blue skies with cumulus clouds and sunshine. That scene in turn whited out. The screen went blank.

"That was session one," Doctor Johnson said. "We're slowly teaching your body to have normal responses."

"Thank you," Jacob said. "It says in the program we do five sessions a day, is it the same every time?"

"The disorder of homosexuality is a tricky one, just like any other disorder, of course, the body and mind have circuitous ways of tenaciously holding on to what they've been accustomed to for so long. In a way, it's a habit, an addiction, like smoking. It takes a lot of reinforcement to reconfigure your responses, and that means that we also have to circumvent the tricks employed by the body and mind as they endeavor to keep your sickness intact. This means that the treatment will have to become more intense, because soon, what you just experienced will become effortless. Therefore, we'll have to graduate to the next level."

"Will you be conducting all my sessions?"

"We have several qualified people on staff. Sometimes I will, yes, sometimes others. But I assure you everybody is well qualified, especially in the spiritual sense."

Jacob took a breather in the lounge. Troy joined him shortly after he had slumped onto one of the lounge sofas.

"So, how was your first go at it?"

Jacob nodded and smiled. "Too soon to say, as I'm sure you'd know. But wow. The process wasn't explained on the web site, I've read about the method elsewhere, here and there. Controversial, understandably. But hey, whatever works, right?"

Troy laughed. "Yes, and it *does* work. Every therapist here is a walkin' testimonial, most are married with children too. I'm about to join the ranks myself, I feel it already, gettin' normal. I welcome the sight of a woman now."

"It's no wonder," Jacob laughed back.

Session two from 11:00 to 13:00 was the same — different but similar videos — all the reactions of intense pain, nausea, and dry heaves contrasted with comfort and relief. Homosexuality equals pain, nausea, vomiting. Heterosexuality equals comfort and relief. The body was learning; soon enough signals would fire through the synapses, rewire his abnormal brain chemistry, and *voila*.

Jacob wasn't very hungry at all for lunch, nausea was still lingering, very slightly. He ate a salad with light dressing, few flakes of pepper, a glass of water.

Session three from 14:00 to 16:00 was an encore of the previous two sessions, different videos. He thought he'd have built up some tolerance to the medication and pain, but no cigar. He chatted with Troy again during his next break, then entered session 4, this time with a different therapist. It was only an hour long, thank goodness, but the responses were all the same. The relief video, while his hands were dipped in warm water and his nausea waned with the efficacious antidote, showed explicit close ups of the inside of the vagina as male hands peeled her mysterious — and once repugnant, frightful — layers open. The gay porn part was different this time. While he fought back vomit and dry heaved, hands freezing, scenes would alternate between naked dudes slamming away and scenes of the twin towers coming down, the debacle of the San Francisco earthquake, and extremely sick men in hospital beds dying of AIDS.

Dinnertime, although he wasn't very hungry again, Jacob ate some of the grilled chicken and slaw. He was joined by Troy and two more outpatients. There wasn't a whole lotta talkin', they all prayed a private prayer before eating.

Group counseling started with an opening prayer led by the counselor, Reed, another ex-homosexual who had beaten the disease, an empathetic survivor. He read aloud from First Corinthians 13 and the session began; two others who hadn't been at dinner joined the group.

"Thank you everybody for joining us tonight, I see we're all here. Ken couldn't be here yesterday but we're all glad to see him here tonight. Group therapy is an integral part of the program where we can share our thoughts and feelings freely. In addition, we have a new member joining us for the two-week inpatient program. Jacob, tell us about yourself."

Everybody clapped and smiled.

"Thanks. I'm Jacob, I'm thirty-one years old, looks like I'm older than half of you here. Um, I'm happy I'm here. I really am. What makes me glad is knowing that I'm not alone, that I'm not suffering from our disorder, this disease alone. I'm originally from Seattle. I was married once, never officially divorced, had two kids, they'd be twelve and six now, I guess. I was very involved with the church until I was caught *in flagrante* as they say. I moved back to the city and stayed there, indulging my disease until September 11 happened. That was when I decided to turn my life around, for real this time."

Everybody nodded in sincere acknowledgment. They all had their stories, of the pain and suffering they had shouldered and continued to shoulder.

"I have horrible memories, a horrible past. But most horrible of all was *me*. I was sick and didn't know it. I thought I was just 'experimenting' with homosexuality, thinking it would just naturally go away. I had a wife, kids, home with two cars. Everything just went *poof*, gone, in a flash. Like a dream, like a desert mirage. I told myself I was an upstanding and respectable member of the community, but I was just self-deceived."

A few of them were wiping tears from their eyes, nodding, empathizing.

"Thank you, Jacob," Reed chimed in. "Your pain is shared by all of us, as we too have suffered from this cursed sickness. Not to diminish the severity of your case, by no means no, but I just want you to know that you are in great company, that every one of us can relate to what you have been through. So thank you, Jacob, for sharing with us. And again, welcome."

"Welcome Jacob," everybody said.

"Thank you everybody. Thank you, my friends."

Everybody there was supportive, strong Christians, on their respective ways to health.

The last session of the day followed the intense yet heart-warming group therapy session. The counselor was the same one who had conducted his fourth session. Scenes on the monitor alternated again; during the pain and nausea the video showed men having gay sex, the September 11 destructions, men having gay sex, the San Francisco earthquake, men having gay sex, AIDS patients dying a slow death, then scenes of a threesome of guys having sex. The scenes played during his stints of physical relief were those of a man, woman, and child enjoying a picnic at a park; the same man, woman, and child standing with hymn books at church, singing Amazing Grace.

From 22:00 to 23:00 Jacob retired to his room for mandatory bible study, prayer, and contemplation of the day's events. Thirteen more days of *this*, Jacob thought to himself. Tempting thoughts of bolting in the middle of the night, never to return, tugged at him. He prayed for the strength to endure, to tough it out to the very end, then he conked out practically on the nose at 23:00 when the electricity in his room was automatically shut off.

III

On day four, the medication was "upped" in strength and the little bit of tolerance he'd acquired was trounced by a nausea that was twice as bad as it had been the first three days. The freezing of the hands was now replaced with heat. Coils wrapped around his hands would heat up just enough to make the tears well up in his eyes but not enough to sear his skin. Naturally the coils would quickly cool when a man and woman were frolicking, kissing, having sex, closeups of her breasts, curves, man's hand running an ice cube down her chest to her stomach, and so on. Heated coils, nausea, vomiting were for dude-on-dude action, closeups of stiff peckers, blowjobs, twin-towers coming down, people dying of AIDS, news scenes of the horrors of homosexual serial killers.

Pain, nausea, vomit: gay, destruction, horror. Relief, comfort, pleasure: heterosexual, bliss, happiness.

The Sunday chapel in the building was packed with the group-therapy crowd and Reed. A local minister came to conduct the service: prayer, hymns, and a sermon. The sermon, big surprise, was on the sodomy-sodomite theme and all its evils as testified to by the bible; anecdotes of homosexual wickedness;

the September 11 event as attributed to god's displeasure against sodomites and liberal politics; the wages of homosexuality as worthy of death. Jacob could have given the sermon himself of course.

On the eighth day, the coils were replaced with electric shocks, delivered to the fingers. The emetic medication was now at maximum potency.

Only five more days, Jacob thought to himself as the day came to a close, he prayerfully pondered his stay at the clinic hitherto. A few newbies had joined the group therapy outpatient program — still no new inpatients — Troy and Ken, cured, had left with a goodbye party and prayer.

Jacob recalled an image of Pat in a an effort to conduct a thought-experiment. The very idea that he had ever done what he had done, with Mikey, Pat, the late, young youth minister, all the one-night stands in Seattle, was astonishing to him now. How absurd and utterly disgusting it all was. How unwell he must have been. It made him feel sick, quite literally, thinking about having had same-sex sex. He went with it. Indeed, the treatments were working. Working wonders.

And thus, at the end of the eighth day, he dared to ponder the idea of making love to a woman. Janet came to mind. Janet. Poor, sweet, simple Janet. No, if he had it to do over again, he wouldn't lose his mind in a blind rage and strangle her, no, her lovely body, her natural perfumes, her hair, lips, bosoms, were comforting to think of now. Of course he could never go back to her or his past ever again. The story of Sodom and Gomorrah had been his metaphor, his impetus, now more so than ever. After he'd been fully cured, he'd seek a new life of faith and service unto the lord, his number-one priority.

13
Ecce Homo

At the end of the fourteenth day, the day before the farewell and congratulatory party to be thrown by Dr. Johnson, therapists, Reed, and other inpatients, Jacob was on cloud nine. Every night since the eighth he'd thought-experimented confirming the fact that the treatment was indeed working. It had proven to be efficacious beyond his wildest hopes, it had been, as Dr. Johnson had said, worth every penny.

His sleep had been solid until the final night. On the fourteenth night he dreamt of walking up the trail of a desert mountain, one that looked like Knobs Hill. Storm clouds were brewing overhead. A crow was perched on a dried, shriveled cactus, staring at Jacob out of two different colored eyes: one grayish blue, the other white. It cawed three times: *Ha Ha Ha* was how it sounded. It spread its wings, flapped them, and folded them back.

"Get out of here you horrible bird," Jacob yelled — why he didn't know — trying to shoo it away.

The crow didn't budge.

"What do you want from me?" Jacob said.

Thunder rumbled; a strong wind began to blow.

The crow stared back, motionless.

Lightning, then loud thunder. A powerful gust of wind knocked him over.

Jacob woke up with a shout, on the floor.

It was the end of December 2003, the city was sparkling with Christmas decorations by day and lights at night. Jacob was well-established, the go-to programmer of Pozo Secos, a side profession that kept him better than afloat. Seven months after he'd completed his treatment at the Calvary Conversion Therapy Center, Jacob had rented a strip-mall space to start the Second Coming Calvary Christian Ministry. At first the Sunday and Wednesday services were primarily attended and supported by the cured ex-homosexuals he'd met during the stint of his two-week inpatient treatment. Troy was one of them. He helped with the advertising campaigns, became the small church's administrator and Jacob's ministry grew.

Within a year's time Jacob's SCCCM was able to move to a church building that he had built. It had been funded by many organizations thanks to member contributions and business donations thanks in part to Troy's helpful marketing legwork. Jacob had regained his footing in the community amongst the well adjusted citizens of god's country, as a proponent of conservative politics, his anti-homosexuality platform being his most aggressively expressed view. Even the mayor of Pozo Secos had become a SCCCM church member. Jacob counseled him in both spiritual and worldly matters.

On July 4 of 2004 Jacob and Troy watched fireworks with the mayor and his family; it was a grand and glorious occasion. They were basking in their successes, having moved up in the world as established, well respected contributors empowered with shaping the spirituality of their community. After the fireworks back at Jacob's brand new six bedroom home they kissed, made out, and made love. Of course they'd felt guilty as hell afterward but were convinced it was nothing but a minor relapse. After all disorders like theirs could sometimes symptomatically rear their ugly heads, even after they'd been cured. It was okay, they were forgiven, they were still healthy, normal, heterosexuals; they pledged to never indulge in the aberrant activities again. The stakes were higher now. So onwards and upwards they went.

In the winter of 2004, the steel workers of the Pozo Secos Mill went on strike in an effort to form a union. As the spiritual advisor to both the Mayor and the Governor of the state, Jacob worked tirelessly to keep their faith strong in the lord, counseled them not give in to the demands of the angry workers. He advised them, with prayer, that god rewards hard work, that when those who work hard become successful, blessed by god, more jobs get created. When more jobs get created, the nation becomes prosperous.

The strike was eventually crushed by the police. The perpetrators — considered medium-security terror threats — were left unemployed and unemployable.

The defeat was a rousing success; Jacob had established himself by championing for lesser government, supporting very well the conservative powers that be. Maybe he'd run for city council one of these days, he thought to himself.

But first, he'd have to find a wife.